With the *Kingdom is Ours*, t and enjoyable insight into the Engl able set of fast play rules provide ooth the novice and veteran players ures of the Bicorne English Civil W.......

The rules have been extensively developed from the author's and friends' house rules. These were purposefully designed to provide a fast, fun and challenging game for wargamers of all abilities, whilst encouraging the education of the readers into the troops and the realities of warfare in the 17th century.

There are many parts to the book in addition to the rules, including an introduction to the Civil War written by Linda Doyle, and a section detailing troop types. This has all been designed alongside the catalogue of Bicorne troops where the reader is encouraged to collect and paint an army of model soldiers, with a view to playing enjoyable wargames with friends. To this end there is a section on how to build up your army if you are new to the period, as well as a scenario to give the reader a good idea of what can be achieved with this fun to play set of rules.

James Carey Daniels was born in Blackpool, Lancashire in 1969. He grew up in a village on the outskirts of Calne in Wiltshire, where he attended the John Bentley School. Subsequently he attended Bath City College – gaining an HND in Electronic Engineering – and then the University of Manchester Institute of Science and Technology, where he graduated with a BSc in Mathematics, Statistics and Operational Research in 1994; he achieved his MBA from the University of the West of England in 1999.

James has been a keen wargamer from the age of 12 and his love of history led to him joining the Sealed Knot Charity aged around 16 – in which he is still an active member. This background, with the pragmatism of an engineer (and combined with the approximation of a statistician), makes James an ideal candidate to write and develop a set of rules based on his experiences and academic knowhow.

James is married to Jennie and they live in Warwickshire with their three children, William, Edward and Henry. This is where they run Bicorne Miniatures as a small family business; he also enjoys playing rugby.

# THE KINGDOM IS OURS

## Fast Play Rules for Wargaming
## The English Civil War Period

## James Daniels

HELION &
COMPANY

Helion & Company Limited
26 Willow Road
Solihull
West Midlands
B91 1UE
England
Tel. 0121 705 3393
Fax 0121 711 4075
Email: info@helion.co.uk
Website: www.helion.co.uk
Twitter: @helionbooks
Visit our blog http://blog.helion.co.uk/

Published by Helion & Company 2016
Designed and typeset by Battlefield Design (www.battlefield-design.co.uk)
Cover designed by Paul Hewitt, Battlefield Design (www.battlefield-design.co.uk)
Printed by Henry Ling Limited, Dorchester, Dorset

Text © James Daniels 2016
Photographs © Jennie Daniels and Charles Singleton 2016
Maps and diagrams © James Daniels 2016

Cover painting by Peter Dennis © Helion & Company Limited 2016

ISBN 978-1-910777-68-8

British Library Cataloguing-in-Publication Data.
A catalogue record for this book is available from the British Library.

All rights reserved. No part of this publication may be reproduced, stored in a
retrieval system, or transmitted, in any form, or by any means, electronic, mechanical,
photocopying, recording or otherwise, without the express written consent of Helion
& Company Limited.

For details of other military history titles published by Helion & Company
Limited contact the above address, or visit our website: http://www.helion.co.uk

We always welcome receiving book proposals from prospective authors.

# Contents

# Author's Introduction and Acknowledgements

Welcome to my first published rules. As with all rules they are probably not perfect; however, please feel free to suggest changes and amendments via the Bicorne Miniatures Facebook Page. These rules are as simple as possible but maintain the flavour of 17th century fighting tactics. The random factors throughout the game place an element of uncertainty in any engagement that should challenge the best of generals! Enjoy your battles!

I would like to take this opportunity to thank my friends in all their contributions to these rules – especially Rowan Edwards, Simon Davies, Linda Doyle, Paul Sturman, Tom Clarke, Sean McLauglin, Jennie Daniels and the rest of Dragon Cottage Wargamers. Finally, I would like to thank Farnborough Wargames Society for the initial rule ideas.

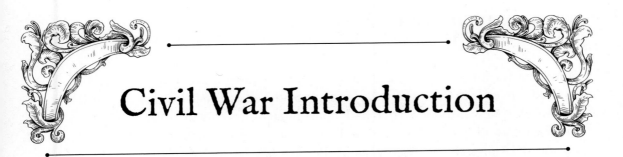

# Civil War Introduction

The period of English Civil Wars was one of the most violent times of English history. It lasted less than 10 years between 1642 and 1651, but it brought chaos, death and destruction and put father against son and brother against brother. Behind it all lay one question: *'Who was to rule the country – King or Parliament?'* These two groups became known as Royalists and Parliamentarians – nicknamed 'Cavaliers' and 'Roundheads'.

By the summer of 1642 the dispute was drifting into civil war and powerful men in every county were taking sides and raising troops, but it was not until King Charles I raised his standard at Nottingham on 22 August that Civil War was openly declared. On that day Lord Brooke was marching his Parliamentary troops towards Coventry and on reaching Southam decided to stay there for the night, while unknown to them, encamped on the other edge of town was the Earl of Northampton with his Royalist forces. Once both sides realised the proximity of the other, they prepared themselves for battle and early the following morning a messy and confused skirmish took place, which after four hours was inconclusive.

Two months later on 23 October 1642 commenced the first of the three major battles – the Battle of Edgehill – and in 1644 came the Battle of Marston Moor and in 1645 the Battle of Naseby. However, a great number of other battles occurred that are frequently overlooked.

King Charles surrendered to a Scottish army in 1646 who eventually handed him over to the English Parliament. By the end of 1648 Oliver Cromwell's New Model Army had consolidated its control over England and King Charles became the first of our monarchs to be put on trial for treason. There was no English law to deal with the situation, so it was written by a Dutch lawyer and based on an ancient Roman law, and the King was executed in London on 30 January 1649.

Oliver Cromwell became Lord Protector in 1653 and for 9 years England was ruled as a republic. However, the monarchy was restored and the King's son was crowned King Charles II on 3 April 1661.

# Battles and Skirmishes of the English Civil War

The following is a list of most of the major battles, sieges and skirmishes that are documented during the English Civil War. This list is not comprehensive and is designed for the reader to do their own research to help when designing scenarios etc. It does, however, show the massive amount of conflict that occurred over this period:

Aberdeen, 1644

Adwalton Moor, 1643

Aldbourne Chase, 1643

Alford, 1645

Alton, 1643

Arundel, 1642, 1643

Auldearn, 1645

Barbados, 1651-2

Basing House, 1643, 1644, 1645

Beacon Hill, 1644

Benburb, 1646

Birmingham, 1643

Boldon Hill, South Shields, 1644

Bolton, 1644

Booth's Uprising, 1659

Bovey Tracey, 1646

Bablylon Hill, 1642

Braddock Down, 1643

Bradford, 1642, 1644

Brentford, 1642

Bridgwater, 1645

Bristol, 1643, 1645

Burton Bridge, 1643

Cadiz, 1656

Carbisdale, 1650

Castle Dore, 1644

Chalgrove Field, 1643

Cheriton, 1644

Chester, 1645, 1646

Chichester, 1642

Clonmel, 1650

Colby Moor, 1645

Colchester, 1648

Cropredy Bridge, 1644

Devizes, 1643, 1645

Donnington Castle, 1644

Dover, 1652

Drogheda, 1649

Dublin, 1646

Dunbar, 1650

Dungan's Hill, 1647

Dungeness, 1652

Dunes, 1658

Edgehill, 1642

Farnham, 1642

Gabbard, the, 1653

Gainsborough, 1643
Galway, 1652
Glencairn's Uprising, 1653-4
Gloucester, 1643
Grantham, 1643
Heptonstall, 1643
Hieton Hamilton, 1650
Highnam, 1643
Hispaniola, 1655
Hopton Heath, 1643
Hull, 1642
Hull, 1643
Inverkeithing, 1651
Inverlochy, 1645
Jamaica, 1655
Jersey, 1651
Kentish Knock, 1652
Kilkenny, 1650
Kilsyth, 1645
Kings Norton, 1642
Knocknaclashy, 1651
Knocknanuss, 1647
Langport, 1645
Lansdown, 1643
Lathom House, (First) 1644
            (Second) 1645
Laugharne Castle, 1644
Launceston, 1643
Leeds, 1643
Leghorn, 1653
Leicester, 1645
Lichfield, Mar 1643
            Apr 1643

Limerick, 1650
Limerick, 1651
Liverpool, 1644
Londonderry, 1649
Lostwithiel, 1644
Lyme, 1644
Macroom, 1650
Maidstone, 1648
Mardyke, 1657
Marshall's Elm, 1642
Marston Moor, 1644
Marston Moor
Meelick Island, 1650
Middlewich (First), 1643
            (Second), 1643
Monte Cristo, 1652
Montgomery, 1644
Nantwich, 1644
Naseby, 1645
Naseby
Newark, 1644
Newark, 1646
Newburn, 1640
Newbury (First), 1643
            (Second), 1644
Olney Bridge, 1643
Ormskirk, 1644
Oswestry, 1644
Oxford campaign, 1644
Pembroke, 1648
Penruddock's Uprising, 1655
Philiphaugh, 1645
Pill, 1644

Plymouth, 1652

Portsmouth, 1642

Portland, 1653

Porto Farina, 1655

Powick Bridge, 1642

Preston, 1648

Rathmines, 1649

Reading, 1643

Ripple Field, 1643

Roundway Down, 1643

Rowton Heath, 1645

St. Fagans, 1648

Santa Cruz, 1657

Scarriffhollis, 1650

Scheveningen, 1653

Scilly Isles, 1651

Seacroft Moor, 1643

Selby, 1644

Severn, 1655

Sherborne, 1642, 1645

Sourton Down, 1643

Southam, 1642

St Fagans, 1648

Stow-on-the-Wold, 1646

Stratton, 1643

Tadcaster, 1642

Taunton, 1645

Tecroghan, 1650

Tenby, 1644

Tippermuir, 1644

Tipton Green, 1644

Torrington, 1646

Turnham Green, 1642

Upton, 1651

Wakefield, 1643

Warrington Bridge, 1651

Waterford, 1649

Waterford, 1650

Wexford, 1649

Weymouth & Melcome, 1645

Wigan Lane, 1651

Winceby, 1643

Winchester, 1642, 1645

Winwick, 1648

Worcester, 1651

York, 1644

# Troops and Weapons of the English Civil War

## Artillery

Artillery consisted of a range of cannon starting from very mobile pieces such as the Scots frame guns up to the enormous Cannon Royal. Both sides used whatever they could get hold of for the battles. For the purposes of these rules the Artillery are classified as follows:

- **Large Guns (Siege guns)** – consisting of the Culverin which fired shots of around 15 pounds up to the enormous Cannon Royal with shots of around 60 pounds.

- **Medium Guns (Field pieces)** – consisting of minions with shots at around 4 pounds, Sakers around 5 pounds and demi-culverins around 9 pounds.

- **Small Guns (Light pieces)** consisting of falcons, falconets and frame guns.

  - **Mortars** – These were of various sizes, however for simplicity in the rules they are all treated the same.

# Infantry

Civil war infantry comprised two distinct types of soldier: pikemen and musketeers. At the beginning of the wars, the most common regimental balance was one pikemen for every musketeer. As the wars progressed the percentage of pikemen declined. By the end of the English Civil War, the ratio of pikemen to musketeers in the New Model Army had reverted to two musketeers to one pikeman.

- **Pikemen** – some were equipped with armour consisting of a helmet, back and breast plate, tassets, and a gorget. The use of armour declined as the civil wars progressed. As well as the 16 to 18-foot pike, the majority of pikemen also carried a short sword (tuck).

- **Musketeers** – would normally be unarmoured and carry a matchlock musket and short sword. Some musketeers were also issued musket rests to support the heavier weapons of the early part of the civil wars.

- **Scots Troops** – Highland troops didn't always conform to the normality of the pikeman or musketeer. Instead they had units of swordsmen, bowmen or axemen. These would be armed with a sword and shield (targe), a bow or the lochaber axe respectively.

# Cavalry

Cavalry units were organised in troops commanded by a captain. Six of these troops were normally brigaded together to form a Regiment commanded by a colonel.

- **Cuirassiers** – were the most heavily armoured of the cavalry, wearing almost full armour into battle. They would normally use pistols, carbines and swords as their main weapons. These troops were a rare sight during the civil wars.

- **Horse or Harquebusiers** – were normally armed with a pair of pistols and a sword, with the officers carrying the carbine or harquebus. These troops would wear a leather buff coat over which they would wear a back and breast plate with gorget and lobster pot type helmet.

- **Dragoons** – were mounted infantrymen who rode small horses to move into position and then fought on foot. They wore no armour and usually carried a musket or carbine and sword. Occasionally there were two mounted on the same horse.

- **Lancers** – the lance was used by Scottish cavalry, particularly in regiments recruited near the border regions. They wore no armour.

# Suggested Equipment Requirements

In addition to your miniature armies you will need the following items.

A playing surface – suggest a 6ft x 4ft table or larger for 28mm figure

Terrain – as per scenarios or see advanced option 1

Tape Measure

Dice – these rules use two types of dice a d6 and a d10.   It is recommended that 10mm dice are used as these will fit in the unit trackers.

Assuming all your dice are of the same size, you will need the following:

- 1 'purple die of dooooom' – or any distinct unique colour that represents the end of turn.

- Enough dice of a single colour to add to the pot for each army's orders. So, 20 red dice for Royalists and 20 yellow dice for Parliament would be a good starting point – you will need more for larger battles. We have found that having different coloured dice per tertio and different colour dice for the General leads to a much more balanced game.

- Different coloured or sized dice to resolve shooting and combats.

- Different coloured dice again to use for marking casualties/ammo/status on the trackers.

- Some D10s for morale and random event tests.

- A dice bag or pot from which to draw the turn die from.

- A protractor to measure those arcs of fire angles.

# Unit Make-Up

What a unit consists of:

All senior officers would have been mounted at this time. Therefore in these rules it is assumed that all Tertio/Brigade commanders are mounted.

Each unit in the 17th century would have normally consisted mainly of rank and file troops along with officers and a colour party. The colour party would have had flags of varying design according to the rank of their officers. The flags, along with the colour of uniform coats, for those that had them, would have helped to identify the unit. Units used to flourish their colours to show who they were and try to cast fear into the enemy. The drummers would also be an important part of the colour party and were used to relay orders by the beat of the drum.

To represent this on the tabletop it looks good to have a selection of figures representing this. So for a unit of pike and shot the following is suggested:

A Pike and Shot Unit Formation

| SHOT | SHOT | PIKE | COMMAND | SHOT | SHOT |
|------|------|------|---------|------|------|
|      |      | PIKE | PIKE    |      |      |

The above diagram shows the pike and shot stands for a standard regiment in Horned Battle formation.

Each unit will have a command base – infantry would normally have a command stand as follows: 1 drummer, 1 standard, 1 officer, and a musician, sergeant or soldier. This would be placed at the centre of the unit and replace one stand of normal troops. Visually very effective

17

and would fight as per the troop type it was part of. For a Pike and Shot unit it will replace 1 stand of Pike and count as a stand of Pike.

Each Cavalry and dragoon unit would also have a cavalry command base consisting of 1 Cornet (flag carrier), 1 officer, 1 musician or additional officer, and a trooper.

The rank and file troops would sometimes have been issued with uniform clothing. These varied with the commanders. It is recommended to do some basic research into the uniform colours of the units you paint if you want to be historically accurate. Google or the Sealed Knot web pages are good places to start.

# Unit Tracking

For these rules to work smoothly, one of the tricks that we found very helpful was to use unit trackers to record things such as turns moved, status, ammunition and casualties. This becomes quite an onerous task using a paper-based system.

To help facilitate this Bicorne has produced a unit tracker (and a General Tracker) that can be used to help with this. It is also possible to make your own.

Unit Identifier - this can be painted in the unit colours or a figure could be added to depict the unit.

Unit status – gives a dice score for whether the unit is:

2. Poor

3. Ordinary

4. Good

5. Excellent

This has a double effect for generals as this is the number of orders remaining and can be reduced as used – remember to reset this at the beginning of each turn.

**Casualties** – This keeps track of the casualties – especially useful for the pike/shot split in foot regiments.

**Turns** – Once a die has been drawn from the cup it can be allocated to the unit being moved – therefore there should be no confusion on how many moves are left etc.

**Ammunition** – this can help keep track of the ammunition; there is room for two dice. Occasionally, random events may increase the ammo available above 12, but you can just balance another die between the two that you're already using.

**Unit status** – this shows whether the unit is in rout or disordered; an alternative way of showing disorder would be to turn the unit marker to 45 degrees.

**Random events** – there can be a lot of things that can impact a unit for a period of d3 turns; these turns can be tracked here.

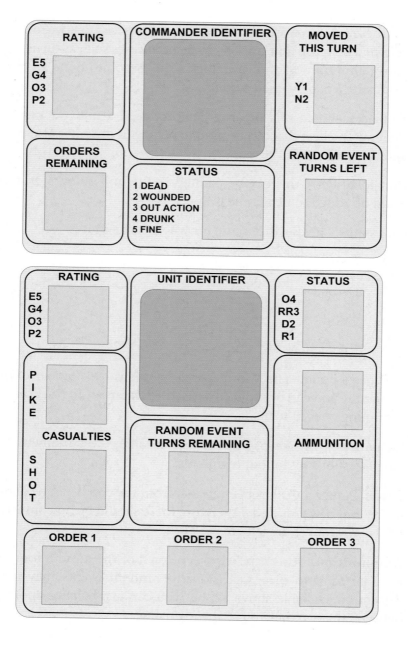

# Bicorne English Civil War Fast Play Rules

Spelling in the 17th century was not regular. We have tried to be consistent, using 'Tertio' rather than 'Tercio' or 'Tertia', etc.; 'Demi Herce' rather than 'Demihearse', 'Demi-Hearse', etc.; 'Horned Battle' rather than 'Horn Battale', etc.; but if we have failed, please accept it as period colour! Terminology was likewise often confusing. We have tried for consistency, but please accept that some words will mean what we want them to mean, no more and no less.

## Army Composition

The Tertio (or Brigade) was the normal army division. Mixing cavalry and infantry was unusual, but in the basic game it is made up as follows:

| | |
|---|---|
| In Tertio | 1 Mounted Tertio Commander<br>2 Horse Regiments<br>3 Foot Regiments<br>1 Saker |
| Horse Regiment | 4 Stands of Horse |
| Foot Regiment | 1 Block of Pike<br>2 Blocks of Shot |
| Pike Block | 4 Stands of Pike |
| Shot Block | 2 Stands of Musket |
| Saker | Medium Gun |
| Stand | 4 figures, 2 wide by 2 deep |

Recommended base sizes (w * d) – A Foot stand is 40mm * 40mm minimum, a Mounted stand is 40mm * 80mm minimum, an artillery stand is 60mm * 80mm minimum, and a Commander stand is 60mm diameter minimum.

If deploying more than 1 Tertio, deploy 1 Mounted Army Commander. Only the Army Commander (the most senior general per side) has additional Order Dice (see **Set Up** and **Orders**) so larger forces have relatively fewer Dice to reflect the difficulty of controlling them.

## Standard Troop Types

### Mounted:

All troops riding horses – Commanders as well as Horse.

Horse – troopers armed with swords and pistols.

### Infantry:

All troops who fought on foot, including dismounted Dragoons, Shot, and Pike.

Shot – Infantry characteristically armed with matchlock or firelock muskets.

Pike – Infantry armed with pike.

Foot – Pike and Shot combined in a single unit.

**Artillery:**

Sakers (Medium Guns) have 4 crew.

# Substituting Troops

The Tertio is the normal command in the basic game – for other scenarios you could add or remove Regiments, or substitute Regiments of Dragoons, Cuirassiers, Lancers, Sword, Bow, Civilians, and different calibre artillery or mortars.  See **Advanced Option 2: Army Selection**.

A Regiment can be exchanged for a Regiment of any other type (but see **Army Selection**, below): the size of Mounted and Infantry Regiments is unchanged (with the exception of Dragoons).  A mob of Civilians can be exchanged for any other Regiment.

Artillery can only be exchanged for other artillery, one large gun for one medium gun or one small gun or a mortar (the better manoeuvrability and arc of fire of smaller pieces offsetting the greater range and hitting power of larger ones).  **Exception**: when using Army Selection, some Armies may have rare or no artillery.  In this case, a gun may be replaced by a Levy unit (8 Stands of Civilians who are -1 on 1642-43 Quality).

### Pike to Shot Ratio

The proportion of Pikes in Royalist and Parliamentarian Foot Regiments tended to fall during the war.  To represent this, Foot Regiments may be of 3 stands of Pike and 6 of Shot (the ideal of 1 to 2 set by Parliament for the New Model Army), 2 Pike and 6 Shot, 1 Pike and 8 Shot, or even 8 Shot.  If no other Regiments in a Tertio have Pike, a single Regiment of 4 to 8 stands of Pike may be fielded.

The number of Infantry figures in the Tertio does not change: any figures left over when these new modelled Regiments are created must form a single 'Forlorn Hope' Regiment of 1 to 7 stands of Shot.

# Permitted Formations

## For all types:

**Line**: 1 stand deep.

**March Order**: 1 stand wide.  Note: units in March Order become disordered if in contact with the enemy.

**Mass**: at least two stands wide, with ranks as near equal as the number of stands permits.

**Schiltron (Square)**: a Mass with the Stands facing outward, sometimes with an empty centre.  Note: units in Schiltron become disordered if they move.

Other formations are only allowed when conforming to terrain.

## Specific to Foot (Pike and Shot) units:

**March Order**: the Pike block between or in front of the two blocks of Shot.

**Demi Herce**: the whole Regiment two stands deep – front stand Shot and rear stand Pike.  (Good for compactness of shooting but not so effective in Melee.)

**Horned Battle**: Block of Pike two or more stands deep with Block of Shot one stand deep on each side.  (Not so compact for shooting but more effective in Melee with the supported Pike bonus.)

**Charge for Horse**: a square with Shot at the corners and Pike, where available, in the centre of each face.  (Be careful where you face your Shot: remember they will fire from that facing.)

# Set Up

## Deployment

Roll a d10 for each Tertio. Tertios are deployed in turn, highest die first.

Each Tertio deploys troops within 6"+1d6" of table edge (Units in March Order may be represented by placing their leading stand on the table: for Units marching in column note their position in the column then enter the table in turn as soon as there is room behind the previous Unit.) and then roll 2d6 for each Commander and each Regiment to determine quality from the Commander & Troop Rating column. Artillery always counts as Good.

| Commander or Regiment Rating | Order Dice (Orders that can be given per Turn per Commander) | Command Radius | Dice Roll (1642-43) | Dice Roll (1644-45) |
|---|---|---|---|---|
| Excellent | 5 | 20" | 12 | 11-12 |
| Good | 4 | 16" | 10-11 | 7-10 |
| Ordinary | 3 | 12" | 6-9 | 4-6 |
| Poor | 2 | 10" | 2-5 | 2-3 |

Command radius is always measured from the outside of the command base.

# Orders

Units must receive an Order Die to act. Order Dice can be given to a Unit through a Commander, reducing the number of Orders remaining to the Commander by 1, or directly to the Unit (it acts on its officers' initiative).

Army Commanders may give Orders to any Unit in their Army. Tertio Commanders may give Orders to any Unit in their Tertio.

Orders may be 'delegated' from Army Commander to Tertio Commander to increase the maximum number of Orders Tertio Commanders can give, which is otherwise limited by their Quality.

Commanders don't require Orders.

The total number of Orders for each Army and Tertio is calculated at the start of each Turn.

## Hard and Easy Orders

It is harder to get Units to obey some orders than others. A unit, unless routing, will always obey easy orders. For hard orders (see below), or when outside Command Radius, a unit Order Test is required.

**Easy Orders:**

- Move;
- Change Formation;
- Fire; and
- Rally from disorder and pursuit – see specific Tests under Rally.

**Hard Orders:**

- Charging and being Charged – see specific Tests under Charge;
- Fire;
- Move, for those units not facing within 30 degrees in a General Advance; and
- Rally from rout – see specific Test under Rally.

### Order Test

Except for the Specific Tests noted above, which have modifiers and a range of results, a unit will carry out an Order on 1d10 with a roll of equal to or greater than:

| Excellent | Good | Ordinary | Poor |
|-----------|------|----------|------|
| 2 | 3 | 4 | 5 |

# General Advance

A Commander may issue a 'General Advance' order (so reducing the number of orders remaining to him) to a specified group of units under his command.  Such a group may be:

- the entire Army;

- an entire Tertio;

- a Tertio without its Artillery;

- all the Cavalry in a Tertio;

- all the Infantry in a Tertio;

- all the Artillery in a Tertio; or

- all the Artillery in an Army if none is more than 4" from the rest.

A General Advance will only affect units in command radius, if another commander is inside command radius then his radius may also be counted.

The Commander specifies the direction of advance. Units facing up to 30° away from this direction make a wheel to the specified direction without delay. Units facing more than 30° away take an Order Test: if they pass they turn to the specified direction but move at half speed.

A single roll is made for movement, using the dice for the slowest moving Troop Type involved. All troops will move at this rate.

Additional Order Dice of the appropriate colour are withdrawn from the pot and one placed for each unit in the group. If there are insufficient Dice remaining in the pot, the enemy player(s) choose which units do not follow the order.

# Turn Sequence:

**Compulsory Moves** – All routing units now lose another stand and make an additional rout move.

**Calculate the number of Orders** - Players must add a number of Dice to a pot or bag equal to one per Unit on the field, plus the number from the Order Dice column above for the Senior Commander (whether a Tertio or Army Commander). Each player should have

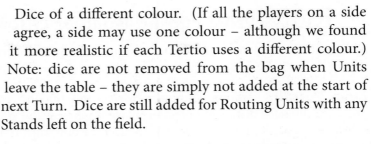

Dice of a different colour. (If all the players on a side agree, a side may use one colour – although we found it more realistic if each Tertio uses a different colour.) Note: dice are not removed from the bag when Units leave the table – they are simply not added at the start of next Turn. Dice are still added for Routing Units with any Stands left on the field.

Additionally, add one die of a different colour, conventionally purple. This is "The Purple Die of Doooom" and when drawn will end the turn.

Players may count the Dice remaining in the pot at any time.

**Orders** – An Order Die is drawn, the colour identifying which player gets to order one of his units (or a Group of them – see **General Advance**). The order may be **Rally, Charge, Move, Change Formation,** or **Fire**. (Note: Melee is not a separate Order – it takes place whenever enemy units are in contact.) When an Order is completed another Die is drawn. It may be that a player gets a number of Orders in a row: such is battle. The chaos of battle means that Orders aren't always received. No one unit may not be given more than 3 Orders per Turn. Any automatic moves, ie Routs and Pursuits, must be determined when they occur.

Units ordered to **Charge** troops may move and fire. Troops with a **Fire** order must stand still and shoot.

**End of Turn** – when "The Purple Die of Doooom" is drawn the turn is over. **All Order and Commanders' Move Indicator dice are removed from the Unit Trays ready for next turn. Any unit and commander status turn trackers are reduced by 1.**

**Events** – ALL players must roll for Events for each of their Commanders, Regiments, and Guns.

# Rally (From Pursuit, Rout Or Disorder)

Roll 1d10 (Commanders must be in their Command Radius to count their Command Bonus).

**From Pursuit.** Troops winning a Melee will initially automatically pursue (rolling for distance) unless the player opts to test to stop them. On subsequent pursuit moves in the same bound the unit must test to see how it feels - modify the Die roll by:

| Ordinary or better Commander | Excellent | Good | Ordinary | Poor | Per Regiment Lost from Tertio | Per Stand Lost |
|---|---|---|---|---|---|---|
| +2 | -1 | +0 | +1 | +2 | -1 | -2 |

On 4 or less Regiment continues pursuit, on a 5-9 Regiment Halts in position Disordered, on a 10+ Halts in Good Order.

**From Rout** - modify the Die roll by:

| Ordinary or better Commander | Excellent/Good | Ordinary | Poor | Pursued | Per Stand Lost |
|---|---|---|---|---|---|
| +2 | +2 | +1 | -1 | -2 | -2 |

On 4 or less – Ooops not this time matey. On 5+, unit halts in place Disordered.

Units will only rally from Rout in response to an order from a Commander.

Units that rally from Rout are permanently disordered: this represents the effect of troops discarding weapons as they run away.

Troops rallying from rout make a half move towards their own base edge.

**From Disorder** – modify the Die roll by:

| Ordinary or better Commander | Excellent | Good | Ordinary | Poor | Per Stand Lost |
|---|---|---|---|---|---|
| +2 | +3 | +2 | +1 | -1 | -1 |

On less than 0 the unit will rout. On 0-2 it remains Disordered. On 3-10 it reforms at the start of the next Turn.

# Charge

## Charge Sequence

The Charging Unit is the Attacker: the unit which is the target of the charge is the Defender.

1. **Charge Declaration** – Units will only charge in response to an order from a Commander. The Attacker must declare its target (it can have only one). Only Cavalry may charge Cavalry. Dragoons may not initiate a charge.

   **Attacking Foot** must declare whether they will Fire into the Defender before they Charge In to melee.

An Attacker can contact a Defender in the flank if the centre of the Attacker's front is behind the line of the Defender's front when declaring the charge: similarly, an Attacker can contact a Defender in the rear if the centre of the Attacker's front is behind the line of the Defender's flank.

2. Defender declares its reaction intent, which, if the charge is successful will be carried out at the end of 6. (see options below).

   - **Foot receiving Cavalry Charge**: Defender may react to being charged by either forming "Charge for Horse" or "Stand and Fire": Foot firing at Charging Cavalry modifies the Die Roll to Hit by -1 to represent the fear caused by the charge.

   - **Cavalry receiving Cavalry Charge**: Defender may react by attempting to "countercharge" into melee. If the Order Test is passed, Defenders move to the Attacker's position at the end of 6. If the Order Test is failed, the attempt to countercharge has failed: Horse (but not Lancers) may Stand and Fire, then the Attacker moves its final distance.

   - **Foot receiving Foot Charge**: Defender may react to being charged by "Standing and Fire". The Defender gets a shot off before melee. Treat as short range.

- **Artillery receiving Charge**: Mortar Crew must "Evade", other Artillery crew may React by "Stand and Fire" or "Evade". Artillery must take an Order Test to fire at short range. Artillery crew may evade moving 3d6" (no Order Test required). If enemy troops interpenetrate (ie overrun) a gun when its crew evade it is spiked and unusable for the rest of the game: there is no movement penalty for spiking the gun.

- **Dragoons**: may react to being charged by either "Stand and Fire" (in which case they must take an Order Test) or "Evade" (no Order Test required).

- **Irregulars**: must always "Evade" (no Order Test required).

- **Commanders:** Commanders cannot be engaged.

3. An Order Test is taken by the declaring unit: this must be passed to initiate the charge – modify the Die Roll by:

| Charging the enemy's rear | Charging the enemy's flank | Own Commander within half Radius | Attacker disordered | Defender disordered | Defending Foot in Good Order | No Ammunition |
|---|---|---|---|---|---|---|
| +2 | +1 | +1 | -1 | +1 | -2 | +1 |

A natural "1" always fails.

4. Attackers determine charge distance: Cavalry = 5d6" (Cuirassiers = 4d6"), Foot = 3d6".

5. **Attacking Foot** moves half charge distance or fires without moving.

   **Attacking Cavalry** moves half charge distance, then Horse (but not Lancers) may fire Pistols into Defender. It sees the result of this Pistol fire and the Defender's response in step 6 before deciding whether to:

   - Retire its remaining charge distance, finishing with its rear to the Defender;

   - Swirl Round Defending Foot, having advanced the remaining charge distance; or

   - Charge In to melee.

   Note: the remaining half move takes place at the end of 7, below.

6. If this first half of the move of the attacking unit places the unit in Stand-to-Stand contact then it is too quick for either unit to fire, change formation, countercharge, or evade! Resolve Melee.

   Otherwise, if the Attacker Charges in, the Defender must take an Order Test to react – modify the Die Roll by:

| Charged in rear | Charged in Flank | Commander within radius |
| --- | --- | --- |
| -2 | -1 | +1 |

Countercharging Cavalry now make their move.

7. All Shooting Hits and Kills are taken now. If Morale Checks are caused they are taken now. If this causes the Attacker to halt, the Attacker retires half the Charge distance taken (ie ¼ the distance rolled) and ends Disordered. If no Morale Checks are caused, or the Checks are passed, move in to Melee.

Failure to contact: If the Attacker fails to contact the Defender, the Attacker becomes Disordered in the position reached. Units charging a building or other obstacle automatically enter if their opponents rout or evade.

An evading unit ends with its back to the enemy.

# When you can initiate and perform a flank attack

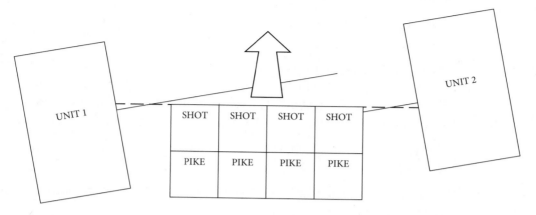

From the above diagram Unit 1 is able to initiate and perform a flack charge as the centre of the unit is behind the target units front line. Unit 2 however cannot instigate or perform a flank attack as although it will hit the enemy unit above in the side it did not start from behind the flank, and in this instance flank attack bonuses cannot be taken.

# When you can initiate and perform a rear attack

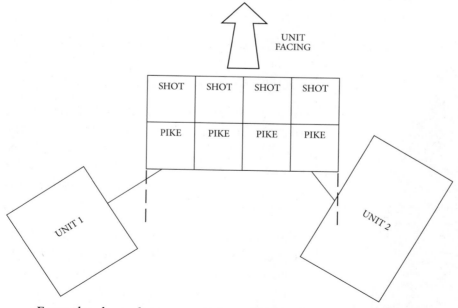

From the above diagram unit 1 would not count a rear attack only a flank attack and unit 2 would count a rear attack.

# Move

| Troop Type | Normal Move | Pursuit/Evade Move | Charge/Rout Move |
|---|---|---|---|
| Foot | 2d6" | 2d6" | 3d6" |
| Cuirassiers | 3d6" | 3d6" | 4d6" |
| Other Mounted and Commanders | 4d6" | 4d6" | 5d6" |
| Small Guns | 2d6" | 2d6" (leaving guns behind) | 3d6" (leaving guns behind) |
| Medium Guns | 1d6" | 2d6" (leaving guns behind) | 3d6" (leaving guns behind) |
| Large Guns | ½d6" | 2d6" (leaving guns behind) | 3d6" (leaving guns behind) |

**Declare Intent:  if a unit is not to move its full distance, it must declare its intent to stop at piece of terrain such as a village or wall, or alongside (not behind) a friendly Unit.**

**Measure a Unit's move distance from the start to the end positions of the furthest moving edge of the unit.**

Commanders can move once, at any point in a Turn, making any number of direction changes without penalty: this does not consume an Order Die. They also get a free move of the minimum distance necessary to get out of the path of a charge.

Roads count as 60mm wide. Note: this allows Artillery on roads, but prevents other types moving 2 stands wide. Bridges and fords are the same width as roads unless otherwise specified.

Regiments of Cavalry and Foot in March Order get a 1d6" bonus to movement in open terrain: this becomes 4" on roads, representing the reduced possibility of nasty surprises. Artillery get a movement bonus of 2" on roads.

Regiments moving in March Order may halt before interpenetrating the Regiment in front. Otherwise, Units ordered to Move must move the full rolled movement distance straight forward, unless before the Move Dice were rolled they declared their intent to stop at a piece of terrain or alongside a friendly unit.

- If this brings it in to contact with enemy there is no "Defensive Fire" (Defender is too surprised) BUT the 'Attacking' Regiment must go in to Melee Disordered.

- If this takes the unit through other friendly unit(s) or Commanders then all units will count as disordered, except Commanders who happily cause disorder but are not affected by it themselves: if the move distance rolled does not allow the moving unit to clear the unit(s) in the way, place it beyond the interpenetrated unit(s) in the direction it is moving.

- Units may drop one stand to the rear without penalty to avoid an obstacle (including other Units) at any time, but must expand this stand back once the obstacle is cleared, also without penalty.

Routers get a free initial turn directly away from the enemy.  A Unit in rout contacted by enemy is dispersed: remove all its Stands from the table.  Units dispersing routers in this way will continue their move and will contact any other Units in their way, fighting enemy and interpenetrating friends.

Pursuit moves must be the full rolled distance even if this disperses troops, disorders friends, ends in contact with another enemy, or leaves the board edge.

Dragoons' dismounted horse holders and horses are dispersed and leave the field if contacted by the enemy.

## Difficult Terrain

Apart from Clear Spaces, Shallow Slopes, Bridges (including causeways, jetties, etc) and Fords, which are clear, and Seas and Lakes, normally impassable, all terrain pieces are normally considered difficult.  However, when setting out terrain any piece may be specified as clear, difficult, or difficult+1, difficult+2, etc, if all players agree. Additional terrain rules can be found on pages 48 and 49.

When a Unit tries to enter such an obstacle roll a d6 for effect, counting +1 if Cavalry, -1 if Irregular Infantry:

| | |
|---|---|
| 1-2 | no delay |
| 3-4 | the unit slows to half speed, and loses any charge bonus |
| 5 | the unit slows to half speed, becomes disordered, and loses any charge bonus |
| 6+ | the unit cannot enter this Turn. |

The unit moves at full speed as soon as its leading stand has cleared the far side of the obstacle.  It dices again each Turn that it tries to move while its leading edge remains within the obstacle.  Linear obstacles such as walls and ditches count a minimum width of 1".  Even if one unit has successfully negotiated an obstacle, it does not necessarily follow that other units will, or indeed that the same unit will if tries to pass back over the same obstacle in the same place!

## Disorder

**Disordered Units move at half speed (except when routing), fire and melee at half strength, -1 on Morale Check. This is cumulative with changing formation, so changing formation reduces movement to quarter distance.**

Troops are in Good Order, ie "standing right in their ranks and files", at the start of the game. They will fall into disorder if their formation is disturbed, either physically or when their morale leaves them unable to hold together.

Troops may regain their Good Order by **Rally From Pursuit** or **Rally From Disorder** or **Events** – Regimental sergeants get shouting. Disorder may be caused by:

| | |
|---|---|
| **Formation** | Contacting Enemy in March Order will disorder the enemy, moving in Schiltron/Square |
| **Rally** | Rally From Pursuit |
| | Rally From Rout |
| **Charge** | Failure to contact in a charge, whether due to morale or lack of move distance |
| **Pursuit** | Failure to contact an enemy in pursuit |
| **Move** | Interpenetrating friends |
| | Difficult Terrain |
| **Kill Rolls** | Burning Buildings |
| **Melee** | Fighting in or against a building |
| **Morale** | Morale Check Result |
| **Events** | The orders don't make sense |

## Change Formation

Formation changes, mounting/dismounting or wheeling to face a different angle from the unit centre, etc reduces movement by half.

Any intent to move after the formation change is complete must be declared, as during Move. If the Order is to change formation and move, and the unit fails its unit Order Test, it will still make its move element from its current position!

# Fire

Range and arcs are measured from the centre front of the block of the firing troop types to the closest point of the unit being fired upon. If this is in range and arc all the stands in a block (or an entire unit) without intervening friends are deemed in range. Each wing of a Horned Battle will fire at ranges determined by its own centre front. Units with two wings firing can only target one enemy, even if this means a wing does not shoot due to fire arcs – blame the officers!

| Range (Inches) | Long (6 to hit) | Medium (5-6 to hit) | Short (3-6 to hit) | Arc (Either side of front) |
|---|---|---|---|---|
| Large Guns | 48" | 32" | 16" | 0° |
| Medium Guns | 36" | 24" | 12" | 10° |
| Small Guns | 24" | 16" | 8" | 20° |
| Shot | 18" | 12" | 6" | 0° |
| Pistols | 9" | 6" | 3" | 90° |
| Darts | 4" | 2" | 1" | 0° |
| Bows | 27" | 18" | 9" | 0° |

## Ammunition

To make the game much more entertaining all missile troops roll 2d6 on their first shot to see how many shots they have in total. Bows subtract 1 and Highland and Irish troops subtract 2 from this roll – which could lead to their ammo being disastrously poor on a double one! Each time the Unit fires reduce the number of shots remaining by one.

## Effect of Fire

Mounted firing from horseback always count as using pistols.

Shot in Charge for Horse formation can fire only where their stands are pointing.

Each Building can fit one Foot or dismounted Dragoon unit. Up to half the firing occupants of the Building can fire from any face at full effect: they may only target one enemy.

Foot cannot move and fire using the same Order.

**Each unit shooting rolls:**

**2d6 per Gun Crew Figure**

**2d6 per Shot Stand**

**2d6 per Horse Stand**

**1d6 per Clansmen Stand**

**In the order below, Change the Dice Rolled by:**

*(Advanced Option 5 only)* Unit undignified: Unit counts as if it has been downgraded e.g. Good becomes Ordinary. Poor will remain poor.

Disordered: half dice.

Artillery at short range (Hail Shot): double dice

**Modifiers per 2 Stands/Artillery Piece if firer:**

| | |
|---|---|
| Excellent/Good +1d6. | |
| Poor -1d6. | |
| Moved, turned, or changed formation in this Turn -1d6. | |
| Artillery: | +1d6 each stand after the first passed through by Roundshot upto a maximum of 4;<br>+1d6 if firing at Cavalry;<br>+1d6 if firing at troops in cover. |

# Kill Rolls:

Kill rolls are made by the attacking player – allowing him to collect those dice that have "hit" and roll them again to cause a "Kill".

| | |
|---|---|
| Foot | 3-6 |
| Cavalry and Artillery | 4-6 |
| Cuirassier | 5-6 |

Modify the Die Roll by:

| Hard Cover | Soft Cover | Bow or Dart |
|---|---|---|
| -2 | -1 | -1 |

A roll of a "6" is always deemed a "Kill".

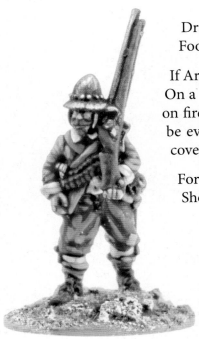

Dragoons are killed as Cavalry whilst mounted and Foot when dismounted.

If Artillery hits troops behind hard cover then roll 1d10. On a 10 the hard cover is destroyed or the building is set on fire for the rest of the game.  Burning Buildings must be evacuated by troops inside who become disordered, cover no longer counts.

For Foot, casualties are allocated randomly to Pike or Shot stands until only one type is left.

| Initial Composition of Regiment | Pike | Shot |
|---|---|---|
| 4 Pike and 4 Shot | 1-3 | 4-6 |
| 3 Pike and 6 Shot | 1-2 | 3-6 |
| 2 Pike and 6 Shot or 1 Pike and 8 Shot | 1 | 2-6 |

Keep track, and when enough casualties of one type (4 figures) have been taken, lose a stand.  When all stands of one type are lost, any excess casualties are carried over to the other type.

# Melee

## Effect of Melee

If a unit is in contact with the enemy all its stands will fight; except routers, who are dispersed.

Units fighting in or against a Building are disordered.

**Each unit in melee rolls:**

**4d6 per Cavalry Stand**

**2d6 per Pike Stand**

**1d6 per Shot Stand**

**1d6 per 3 Gun Crew Figures (rounding up, eg for 4 Crew roll 2d6)**

**In the order below, Change the Dice Rolled by:**

*(Advanced Option 5 only)* Unit undignified: Unit counts as if it has been downgraded e.g. Good becomes Ordinary. Poor will remain poor.

Disordered: half Dice.

Charging, unless crossing cover or Cavalry charging against foot in Charge for Horse in good order: double Dice.

Counter Charging Cavalry, unless crossing cover: double Dice.

Cavalry fighting disordered Foot, or in the second Round of a Melee when pushing back Foot: double Dice.

**Modifiers per Stand if:**

| | |
|---|---|
| Pike fighting in the front rank against Foot, supported by Pike in Good Order directly behind them | +2d6 |
| Attacking in rear | +2d6 |
| Attacking in flank | +1d6 |
| Upslope of opponents | +1d6 |
| Fighting enemy while pursuing | +1d6 |
| Infantry with Sword, or Bill, as their main arm charging | +1d6 |
| Infantry with Sword as their main arm fighting Infantry Unit without Pike or Bill | +1d6 |
| Foot attacking a Regiment in "Charge for Horse" (note: "Charge for Horse" has no Flank or Rear) | +1d6 |
| Mounted Dragoon | -1d6 |
| Excellent or Good | +1d6 |
| Poor | -1d6 |

**Melee Results: hit on 5-6, Kill Rolls as per Firing. Units with most casualties lose, Units with equal casualties draw: see Morale.**

| | |
|---|---|
| Foot | 3-6 |
| Cavalry and Artillery | 4-6 |
| Cuirassier | 5-6 |

Modify the Die Roll by:

| Hard Cover | Soft Cover |
|---|---|
| -2 | -1 |

A roll of a "6" is always deemed a "Kill".

If the units remain in contact after Melee then the next Round of fighting is done immediately. If either side routs, the other will pursue unless they choose to roll under **Rally from Pursuit**. If pursuers contact fresh enemy, this is counted as a continuation of the original melee. This continues until ALL contact between enemy figures is broken, when another Order Die is drawn.

When a defending unit in cover loses a melee then the cover is assumed to be breached – no cover bonus for the subsequent rounds of Melee.

Once dismounted Dragoons are routed it is assumed that the cowardly handlers are long gone with the horses and they will no longer be able to remount during the game – even if they rally!

# Morale

**A Morale Check should be taken immediately when:**

Artillery Crew falls to half strength or less.

1 stand of casualties lost from Regiment or Mob.

Unit loses or draws melee.

Commander in chain of command killed.

If any of these events occur together (eg lost a stand and lost melee) then only one Morale Check is done.

**Roll 1d10. Modify the Die roll by:**

| | |
|---|---|
| Army Commander or Commander of the Unit's Tertio is in Command Radius and is: Excellent | +2 |
| Good | +1 |
| Poor | -1 |
| Unit is: Excellent | +2 |
| Good | +1 |
| Poor | -1 |
| Won melee | +2 |
| Lost melee | -1 |
| Unit is disordered | -1 |
| Per stand lost in total | -1 |
| Artillery: per crew lost in total | -1 |
| Flank attacked | -1 |
| Rear attacked | -2 |
| Each unit in Tertio lost/routing or outside command radius | -1 |

**Result:**

| | |
|---|---|
| 2 or less | unit routs: if in melee move directly away from enemy, if not directly towards own base edge |
| 3-4 | fall back full move facing enemy then disordered (if in rout continue routing) |
| 5-6 | hold in position disordered |
| 7 or more | continue in Good Order. |

# Events Test

On drawing "The Purple Die of Doooom" Roll 1d10 for each unit and each Commander, on a result of 9 or 10, roll 2d10 on the following Chart (for Commanders, a Tertio or Regiment is selected randomly from their command):

| | |
|---|---|
| 2 | Oh Dear – Regiment decides it's time to go home – unit routs. |
| 3 | Disaster strikes – lose one stand of troops from the Regiment (and take a Morale Check). |
| 4 | Poor powder – lose d6 shots (if unit has not already fired then roll for ammo now as normal less 1d6). |
| 5 | Tertio or Army Commander hit, Roll a d6: 1-4 Tertio Commander; 5-6 Army Commander (unless it was a Commander testing, then it would be that Commander!) - see chart below. |
| 6 | Sir Gilbert is drunk again! Remove 3 Order Dice for D3 Turns. Note: cumulative in both Dice, up to a maximum of the Commander's Order Dice, and Turns. |
| 7 | Heavy smoke covers front of Regiment for D3 Turns. Half fire Dice, move/charge at half speed, count Soft Cover. This smoke will follow the Regiment around for the duration. |
| 8 | Downgrade –  if already Poor, take an immediate Morale Check. |
| 9 | The orders don't make sense. Regiment is now disordered. |
| 10 | Regiment is dismayed and must retire a normal move away from enemy now. They remain in Good Order facing the enemy. |
| 11 | Regiment gets all excited and must advance a normal move towards the enemy now. |
| 12 | Powder replenishment – gain additional d6 powder for one regiment. |
| 13 | Upgrade – if already Excellent then they may make a free move now. |
| 14 | Exceptional Ammunition – for this units next shot in the next turn only (if it is able) double dice before modifiers |
| 15 | Regimental sergeants get shouting – all disordered Regiments in Tertio are now in Good Order; Routers rally but remain Disordered. |
| 16 | Rally back 1 stand to a Regiment in your Tertio. |
| 17 | Rally back 1 stand to a Regiment in your Army |
| 18 | General Advance – all Regiments in the Tertio advance forwards ½ move now. |
| 19 | Any lost Regiment (or lost artillery piece) is brought on as reinforcements at the board edge centre of player's deployment zone. |
| 20 | Reinforcements!  Bring on a new unit of your choice (not rare) at the board edge centre of player's deployment zone. |

# Commander Hit Chart

Roll 2d6, effect as follows (Don't forget to roll Morale Checks!):

| | | |
|---|---|---|
| 2-5 | **'E's not pinin', e's passed on!** This Commander is no more! He has ceased to be! E's expired and gone to meet his maker! E's a stiff! Etc...... | **Roll for new Commander after d3 Turns.** |
| 6-9 | **Mortal Wound!** All right, we'll call it a draw. Oh, oh, I see – running away then! Come back here and take what's coming to you! I'll bite your legs off! | **Fights on for d3 Turns, then roll immediately for new Commander.** |
| 10-11 | **It's only a flesh wound!** Commander calls for the barber surgeon. | **Out of action for d3 Turns.** |
| 12 | **'Tis but a scratch!** Commander fights on, earning the admiration of his troops. | **Random Regiment under his command is inspired and is upgraded.** |

# Advanced Option 1: Terrain

Players are encouraged to choose terrain acceptable to all concerned, for example representing a historical battlefield or suitable for an agreed scenario.

Otherwise, chose a set of 16 terrain pieces (this seems to work for a normal size table – select more or less for a particularly large or small playing area). A piece can be any size as long as both sides agree.

Pieces are placed alternately. Nominate one side A and the other B, and roll 1d6 to see who places the first piece: 123, side A; 456, side B.

Each side then choses a piece from the set in the following order, so all Water is placed before any Route, all Routes are placed before any Slopes, and so on.

| 1st | Water (eg sea, lake, river, canal, stream, marsh, bog, or soft ground) |
|-----|-----|
| 2nd | Path, track, road, or similar route; which can cross water (eg by ford, bridge, or causeway) |
| 3rd | Slopes (shallow slopes can be placed under roads and flowing water – but not seas or lakes!) |
| 4th | Buildings, walls, hedges, broken ground, banks, minor fortifications (eg earth bastions, ditches, or trenches) |
| 5th | Vegetation (eg crops, woods, forest, or vineyards) |
| 6th | Near-impassable obstacles: crags, cliffs, major fortifications (eg stone curtain walls and towers) |

Routes and Shallow Slopes are normally clear:  Seas, Lakes, Canals and Crags are difficult+5 (ie impassable without special equipment – boats, scaling ladders, ropes, etc).  Other terrain pieces are normally difficult (see **Difficult Terrain**).  However if both sides agree a piece may count as clear ground or be more difficult (+1, +2 etc).  A piece may have more than one level of difficulty, for example a slope may be mostly gentle but have a craggy area.  The placing side proposes the difficulty of the piece: if the other side does not agree it will be normal.

Once all pieces are placed, each side can remove up to 2 pieces.

Pick a long edge.  Roll 1d6 to see which side deploys on that edge: 123, side A; 456, side B.

# Advanced Option 2: Army Selection

Players will no doubt field whatever army they want.  However we recommend that armies be one of:

- Royalist

- Early Parliament

- New Model Parliament

- Scots Covenant

- Scots Royalist (Montrose)

- Irish (Confederate).

Mixed armies are permitted: in particular a Scots Covenant Tertio in a New Model army, an Irish Tertio in a Royalist army (or vice versa), or a New Model Tertio (representing Eastern Association) in an Early Parliament army.

Note: In spite of the make up of the basic Tertio in these rules, historically Tertios did not normally contain both Cavalry and Infantry.

## Additional Troop Types

Irregular – troops expected to prefer a running fight who will evade and return, and see no shame in avoiding melee. (As opposed to Regular troops expected to stand and fight, who run away only when their morale fails.)

**Mounted:**

All troops riding horses, including mounted Dragoons and Commanders as well as Cavalry.

Dragoons – Shot mounted on horses, 4 stands to a regiment whilst mounted, gain an additional two stands to the Regiment when dismounted, loose two stands when mount up. Normally fight dismounted: while mounted count -1d6 per stand in Melee, move as Cavalry.

Cavalry – troops who normally fight mounted, including Horse, Lancers, and Cuirassiers.

Horse – the most common sort of Cavalry, armed with swords and pistols and wearing back and breast and buff coats when available.

Cuirassiers – Horse with more complete armour: Roll to Kill 5-6, normal move 3d6", charge move 4d6".

Lancers – Cavalry with few or no pistols, carrying lances: count +1d6 per stand when charging.

**Infantry:**

All troops who fought on foot, including dismounted Dragoons, Foot, Shot, Pike,

Sword, Bow, Bill, and Civilians.

Shot – Infantry characteristically armed with matchlock or firelock muskets.

Pike – Infantry armed with pike (long spears carried two-handed).

Foot – the most common form of Infantry, with Pike and Shot combined in a single unit.

Clansmen – Highland and Ulster Scots armed with a mixture of weapons including Swords. Count as Shot but with reduced numbers shooting.

Bow – Shot armed with bows instead of musket: longer-ranged than other Shot but with a reduced chance of killing. Many have Swords.

Bill – Infantry armed with long-staved axes, including bills, glaives, and halberds: count as Sword but fight 2d6 per Stand in melee. Replace Pike in Pike and Shot units.

Civilians (peasants, townsfolk and other mostly untrained individuals, such as Clubmen, Levellers, and Levies) – raw, poorly armed, but often enthusiastic Infantry who are at best pretty ineffectual so form a Mob of 16 stands: count as Shot in Melee but lack the training, ammunition, and weapons to shoot.

Levy – represents troops who would much rather be elsewhere, including the dregs of Highland Clans. They are equivalent to Civilians but count -1 on 1642-43 Quality, but form in Units of 8 Stands.

Swords – Infantry (see Bow and Clansmen) armed with edged weapons including axes and long knives count as +1d6 per stand if charging.

### Artillery:

Large Guns (Demi-Cannon and Cannon) have 6 crew.

Medium Guns (Saker, Demi-Culverin, and Culverin) have 4 crew.

Small Guns (Frame Gun, Minion, Falconet, and Falcon) have 3 crew.

Mortar – a short-barrelled Gun with 3 crew: Mortars count as small guns except they have a 90 degree arc of fire, cannot fire at short range, and if charged must evade.

**Draft:**

Wagons, Baggage and other paraphernalia pulled by draft animals. Move at Foot speed.

# Troop Type Availability

In the Troop Type Availability Table, the availability of troops is described as:

| | |
|---|---|
| Unavailable | the Army can't have them |
| Rare | up to one per Army |
| Scarce | up to one per Tertio |
| Common | any number |
| Predominant | at least half the Army |

| Troop Type | Availability |
|---|---|
| Cuirassiers | rare in Royalist and Early Parliament Armies; unavailable in all others. |
| Horse | common in England; scarce in Ireland; scarce in early and unavailable in later Scots Covenant Armies; rare in early and scarce in later Montrose's Scots Royalist Armies. |
| Lancers | scarce in Covenant Armies (where they may be in combined units with Horse); unavailable in England except in Northern Royalist Armies, where they were rare; unavailable in Ireland outside Ulster, where they were scarce (replacing Horse 1:1); unavailable in early and rare in later Scots Royalist Armies (replacing Horse 1:1). |
| Dragoons | scarce in Parliament Armies; rare in Royalist, Covenant, and Irish Armies; unavailable in early and rare in later Scots Royalist Armies. |

| Troop Type | Availability |
|---|---|
| Foot | predominant in Scots Covenant and Irish Armies; common in England; scarce in Scots Royalist Armies. |
| Irish or Highland Foot | common in Scots Royalist and Irish Armies; rare in Scots Covenant Armies; unavailable in England. |
| Clansmen | predominant in Ulster (replacing Foot 1:1); scarce elsewhere in Ireland; common in Scots Royalist Armies; rare in Scots Covenant Armies; unavailable in England. |
| Bill | rare in Royalist Armies (replacing all Pike in one Regiment); unavailable in all others. |
| Bow | rare in Scots Royalist Armies (may be in combined units with Clansmen) ; unavailable in all others. |
| Artillery | scarce in English and Scots Covenant Armies, rare and limited to Light Guns in Scots Royalist Armies, rare in Irish Confederate Armies. |
| Civilians | always rare on battlefields, especially after the fighting started! |
| Wagons | scarce in all Armies |

# Advanced Option 3: Troop Characteristics

Some troops had characteristic behaviours, which we represent by special factors. In each case we have tried to balance advantages and disadvantages, even where this stretches what we know somewhat: for example the advantage in ammunition for Early Parliament Horse and New Model Foot could reasonably be extended to all Parliament troops.

| Type | Advantage | Disadvantage | Reason |
|------|-----------|--------------|--------|
| Bow | Longer ranged than Shot; roll a d6 at the start of the game – on 4 or more have swords/ axes. May evade. | Effect: -1 on Kill Roll; Ammunition: -1 shots. -1 to charge or countercharge. | Reflects their ability to engage targets at long range, the possibility of them carrying cutting weapons, the lower penetration of bows relative to muskets, and the difficulty of obtaining sufficient arrows in the age of gunpowder. By this date, Bow were Irregular Troops who saw no shame in avoiding melee. |
| Clansmen | Always have Swords. May countercharge Infantry | Only some have Muskets and Bows – 1d6 per stand. +1 on Order Test to Rally from Pursuit; Ammunition: -2 Shots. | Reflects the probability of them carrying cutting weapons (and tendency to get stuck in) and their often critically poor supply. |
| Irish Confederate | Free mob of Civilians or Regiment of Sword. | Always count as 1642-43. | Reflects their popular support but lack of experience. |
| Early Parliament Horse | +2 Shots. | -1 on Order Test to Countercharge; cannot Charge In on a score of 7 on their Morale Check to Charge. | Reflects their tendency to shoot instead of charge. |
| New Model Horse | +2 on Order Test to Rally from Pursuit, once during a game can recover a lost stand to a Regiment when rallying from pursuit. | -1d6 on Charge Move (so charge 4d6"). | Reflects their ability to rally and charge again and their training to charge at the trot instead of the gallop. |

| Type | Advantage | Disadvantage | Reason |
|---|---|---|---|
| New Model Foot (except Eastern Association) before mid-1645 | +2 Shots. | -1 when rolling for quality. | Reflects their better finance and supply, but lesser experience until after Naseby. |
| Royalist Horse | +1 on Morale Check to Charge; +1 on Order Test to Countercharge. | +1 on Order Test to Rally from Pursuit; Ammunition: -1 Shots. | Reflects their high morale, indiscipline, propensity to looting and relatively poor finance and supply. |
| Royalist Cornish Foot in 1643 (1 Tertio only) | Count as 1644-45 for Quality. | Ammunition: -1 Shots. | Reflects their high morale but relatively poor finance and supply. |
| Scots Royalist | Army Commander Quality is always Excellent. | -1 unit per army. | Reflects Montrose's ability to get the best from his army on the battlefield – and his perpetual lack of numbers. |
| Veteran Royalist Foot from late 1644 until mid-1645 | +1 for Quality. | Ammunition: -1 Shots. | Reflects their greater experience but inferior finance and supply until Naseby - after which they no longer existed. |
| Border Horse | May evade. | -1 to charge or countercharge. | Irregular Troops who saw no shame in avoiding melee. |
| Up to half Clansmen | May evade. | -1 to charge or countercharge. | Irregular Troops who saw no shame in avoiding melee. |
| Irregular Ulster Clansmen | May use Darts. | Ammunition: -2 Shots. | Reflects the difficulty of carrying large numbers of oversized arrows! |
| Scots Covenant Shot | Roll a d6 at the start of the game – on 5 or more the Shot have Swinefeathers. (Count as Stakes.) | Ammunition: -1 Shot. | Because they sometimes used them. |

# Advanced Option 4: Battalia

Battalia are Regiments grouped together. They can be formed before the start of the game, or at any time during it using a Commander's Order to **Change Formation**. Detaching one or more Regiments from a Battalia also requires the Commander to issue a **Change Formation** order.

Once the Battalia is formed it is treated exactly like any other Regiment, needing one die per order.

Battalia are made up of a number of regiments. Instead of taking morale tests when they lose one stand and counting -1 per stand lost, they test morale when they lose one stand *per regiment in the Battalia* and count -1 for each stand *per regiment.*

Eg, a 4-regiment Battalia loses 3 Stands to shooting. It does not test morale. It then loses a stand in melee. This takes it up to 4 Stands so it must now test.

If it has lost 7 Stands in all, it takes, -1, not -7, on morale. When it loses 8 Stands it will count -2.

# Advanced Option 5:
# Troops leaving the table in Pursuit

Occasionally troops may get carried away and leave the table in pursuit of the enemy. Troops that leave the table have a chance of returning after d3 turns during the compulsory rout moves phase. Once that turn is up the unit may return from the point at which it left on a roll of a 4 or more on a d6, else it is counted as lost in pursuit.

# Advanced Option 6:
# Preserving the Dignities

The Drill Books of the period argue strongly for putting your best man at the right front of your block, and then describe a complicated system of file leaders, file closers, half file leaders, and so on. In short, every soldier had his particular place in the formation. These are the Dignities. Units where the dignities have not been preserved are 'undignified' (joke).

To use Dignities in the game, mark the right hand (senior) and left hand (junior) Stand of each unit. These Stands must be at the right front and left rear of every formation. The effect of this is to make some turns and formation changes much quicker than others. To represent the importance placed on Preserving the Dignities, units other than Mobs take a penalty (downgrade for Fire and Melee) when they are undignified, ie when these stands are in the wrong positions.

The distance moved to get the corners in the correct position is deducted from the move distance – it may sometimes take more than one Order to prevent units being undignified.

**Regiment in March Order with Dignities:**

**Facing Left to form Line with Dignities: a quick turn: the corners just move the depth of the Stand.**

**Facing Right to form Line with Dignities: not so quick: the corners move the width of the whole unit.**

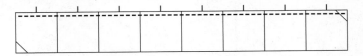

**Pike and Shot Units** have both Pike and Shot dignities marked. This allows them to form Demi Herce and Horned Battle with Dignities. It also allows March Order with Pike leading or with Shot leading **and** trailing.

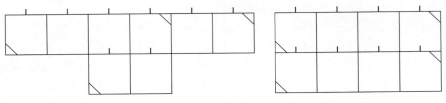

Tertios – and armies – should respect dignities, however sometimes officers get it wrong!  If the dignities are not in the correct position for the formation then the unit is counted as undignified.  Movement must be used to regain dignity.

Complicated drill movements are recommended to keep each soldier in the right place. To turn the block to the rear, for example, the officer is recommended to open spaces between files, then countermarch: i.e. have each man in the old front rank turn to his right and march between the files followed by the men behind him until the whole block faces to the rear.  However that reverses the soldiers' positions in the ranks, so then the unit is turned to its flank, countermarched again, and finally turned to the (new) front and the gaps between files closed.  Not surprisingly, this is a much slower process than having each soldier simply turn about where he stands.

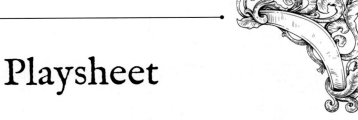

# Playsheet

| Set Up | | | | |
|---|---|---|---|---|
| **Commander or Regiment Rating** | **Order Dice** | **Command Radius** | **Dice Roll (1642-43)** | **Dice Roll (1644-45)** |
| Excellent | 5 | 20" | 12 | 11-12 |
| Good | 4 | 16" | 10-11 | 7-10 |
| Ordinary | 3 | 12" | 6-9 | 4-6 |
| Poor | 2 | 10" | 2-5 | 2-5 |

| Turn Sequence: | |
|---|---|
| 1) | Compulsory Moves |
| 2) | Calculate the number of Orders and put the relevant dice into the cup |
| 3) | Draw dice to issue Orders – Turn Over with "The Purple Die of Dooooom" |
| 4) | Roll for Events |
| 5) | Start Next Turn |

| Rally (From Pursuit, Rout or Disorder) – Roll 1d10 | | | | | |
|---|---|---|---|---|---|
| **From Pursuit:** | | | | | |
| Ordinary or above Commander | Excellent | Good | Ordinary | Poor | Per Regiment Lost from Tertio |
| +2 | -1 | 0 | +1 | +2 | -1 |
| On 4 or less pursues, on a 5-9 Regiment Halts in position Disordered, on a 10+ Halts in Good Order. | | | | | |
| **From Rout:** | | | | | |
| Ordinary or above Commander | Excellent or Good | Ordinary | Poor | Pursued | Per Stand Lost |
| +2 | +2 | +1 | -1 | -2 | -2 |
| On 4 or less – Ooops not this time matey. On 5+, unit halts in place Disordered. | | | | | |
| **From Disorder:** | | | | | |
| Ordinary or above Commander | Excellent | Good | Ordinary | Poor | Per Stand Lost |
| +2 | +3 | +2 | +1 | -1 | -1 |
| On less than 0 the unit will rout. On 0-2 it remains Disordered. On 3-10 it reforms at the start of the next Turn. | | | | | |

Please visit www.helion.co.uk to download this Playsheet in PDF format.

## Firing

| Range (Inches) | Long (6 to hit) | Medium (5-6 to hit) | Short (3-6 to hit) | Arc (Either side of front) |
|---|---|---|---|---|
| Large Guns | 48" | 32" | 16" | 0° |
| Medium Guns | 36" | 24" | 12" | 10° |
| Small Guns | 24" | 16" | 8" | 20° |
| Shot | 18" | 12" | 6" | 0° |
| Pistols | 9" | 6" | 3" | 90° |
| Darts | 4" | 2" | 1" | 0° |
| Bows | 27" | 18" | 9" | 0° |

Each unit shooting rolls:

| 2d6 per Gun Crew Figure | 2d6 per Shot Stand | 2d6 per Horse Stand | 1d6 per Clansmen Stand |
|---|---|---|---|

In the order below, Change the Dice Rolled by:

*(Advanced Option 5 only) Unit undignified: Unit counts as if it has been downgraded.*
Disordered: half dice.
Artillery at short range (Hail Shot): double dice

Modifiers per 2 Stands/Artillery Piece if firer:

| | |
|---|---|
| Excellent/Good | +1d6 |
| Poor | -1d6 |
| Moved, turned, or changed formation in this Turn | -1d6 |
| Artillery: short range (Hail Shot) | Double Dice |
| Artillery: +1d6 each stand after the first passed through by Roundshot upto a maximum of 4 | +1d6 (max 4) |
| Artillery: Firing at Cavalry | +1d6 |
| Artillery: Firing at troops in cover | +1d6 |

## Kill Rolls:

| By the attacking player: | |
|---|---|
| Foot | 3-6 |
| Cavalry and Artillery | 4-6 |
| Cuirassier | 5-6 |
| Modify the Die Roll by: | |
| Hard Cover | -2 |
| Soft Cover | -1 |
| Bow or Dart | -1 |

## Move

| Troop Type | Normal Move | Pursuit/Evade Move | Charge/Rout Move |
|---|---|---|---|
| Foot | 2d6" | 2d6" | 3d6" |
| Cuirassiers | 3d6" | 3d6" | 4d6" |
| Commanders and Cavalry | 4d6" | 4d6" | 5d6" |
| Small Guns | 2d6" | 2d6" (leaving guns behind) | 3d6" (leaving guns behind) |
| Medium Guns | 1d6" | 2d6" (leaving guns behind) | 3d6" (leaving guns behind) |
| Large Guns | ½d6" | 2d6" (leaving guns behind) | 3d6" (leaving guns behind) |

| Morale | |
|---|---|
| **A Morale Check should be taken immediately when:** | |
| Artillery Crew falls to half strength or less. | |
| 1 stand of casualties lost from Regiment or Mob. | |
| Unit loses or draws melee. | |
| Commander in chain of command killed. | |
| **Roll 1d10.  Modify the Die roll by:** | |
| Army Commander or Commander of the Unit's Tertio is in Command Radius and is Excellent | +2 |
| Army Commander or Commander of the Unit's Tertio is in Command Radius and is Good | +1 |
| Army Commander or Commander of the Unit's Tertio is in Command Radius and is Poor | -1 |
| Unit is Excellent | +2 |
| Unit is Good | +1 |
| Unit is Poor | -1 |
| Won melee | +2 |
| Lost melee | -1 |
| Unit is disordered | -1 |
| Per stand lost in total | -1 |
| Artillery: per crew lost in total | -1 |
| Flank attacked | -1 |
| Rear attacked | -2 |
| Each unit in Tertio lost/routing or outside command radius | -1 |

| Result: | |
|---|---|
| 2 or less | unit routs: if in melee move directly away from enemy, if not directly towards own base edge |
| 3-4 | fall back full move facing enemy then disordered (if in rout continue routing) |
| 5-6 | hold in position disordered |
| 7 or more | continue in Good Order. |

| Difficult Terrain | |
|---|---|
| When a Unit tries to enter such an obstacle roll a d6 for effect, counting +1 if Cavalry, -1 if Irregular Infantry: | |
| 1-2 | no delay |
| 3-4 | the unit slows to half speed, and loses any charge bonus |
| 5 | the unit slows to half speed, becomes disordered, and loses any charge bonus |
| 6+ | the unit cannot enter this Turn. |

| Order Test | | | |
|---|---|---|---|
| Carry out Order on d10 with a roll of equal to or greater than: | | | |
| Excellent | Good | Ordinary | Poor |
| 2 | 3 | 4 | 5 |

| Melee |
|---|
| **Each unit in melee rolls:** |
| 4d6 per Cavalry Stand   2d6 per Pike Stand   1d6 per Shot Stand   1d6 per 3 Gun Crew Figures (rounding up) |
| In the order below, Change the Dice Rolled by: |
| *(Advanced Option 5 only) Unit undignified: Unit counts as if it has been downgraded.* |
| Disordered: half Dice. |
| Charging, unless crossing cover or Cavalry charging against foot in Charge for Horse in good order: double Dice. |
| Counter Charging Cavalry, unless crossing cover: double Dice. |
| Cavalry fighting disordered Foot, or in the second Round of a Melee when pushing back Foot: double Dice. |

| **Modifiers per Stand if:** | |
|---|---|
| Pike fighting in the front rank against Foot, supported by Pike in Good Order directly behind them | +2d6 |
| Attacking in rear | +2d6 |
| Attacking in flank | +1d6 |
| Upslope of opponents | +1d6 |
| Fighting enemy while pursuing | +1d6 |
| Infantry with Sword as their main arm charging | +1d6 |
| Infantry with Sword as their main arm fighting Infantry Unit without Pike or Bill | +1d6 |
| Foot attacking a Regiment in "Charge for Horse" (note: "Charge for Horse" has no Flank or Rear) | +1d6 |
| Mounted Dragoon | -1d6 |
| Excellent or Good | +1d6 |
| Poor | -1d6 |

**Melee Result: hit on 5-6, Kill Rolls as above.  Units with most casualties lose, Units with equal casualties draw.**

| Charge Sequence |
|---|

1.    Charge Declaration

2.    Defender declares its reaction intent

3.    An Order Test is taken by the declaring unit using the following modifiers:

| Charging rear +2 | Charging flank +1 | Commander in half Radius +1 | Attacker disordered -1 | Defender disordered +1 | Foot Charging Foot in Good Order -2 | No Ammunition +1 |
|---|---|---|---|---|---|---|

A natural "1" always fails.

4.    Attackers determine charge distance

5.    Attacking Foot moves half charge distance or fires without moving.

  Attacking Cavalry moves half charge distance, then Horse may fire Pistols into Defender. It will then choose:

- to retire its remaining charge distance, finishing with its rear to the Defender;
- to swirl Round Defending Foot, having advanced the remaining charge distance; or
- to charge in to melee.

6.    If this first half of the move of the attacking unit places the unit in Stand-to-Stand contact - resolve Melee

Otherwise, if the Attacker Charges in, the Defender must take an Order Test to react – modify the Die Roll by:

| Charged in rear -2 | Charged in Flank -1 | Commander within radius +1 |
|---|---|---|

7.    All Shooting Hits and Kills are taken now. If Morale Checks are caused they are taken now.  If this causes the Attacker to halt, the Attacker retires half the Charge distance taken (ie ¼ the distance rolled) and ends Disordered.  If no Morale Checks are caused, or the Checks are passed, move in to Melee.

Failure to contact: If the Attacker fails to contact the Defender, the Attacker becomes Disordered in the position reached.  Units charging a building or other obstacle automatically enter if their opponents rout or evade.

**Events Test – Roll 1d10 for each unit and Commander, on a result of 9 or 10, roll 2d10 on the following Chart:**

| | |
|---|---|
| 2 | Oh Dear – Regiment decides it's time to go home – unit routs. |
| 3 | Disaster strikes – lose one stand of troops from the Regiment (and take a Morale Check). |
| 4 | Poor powder – lose d6 shots (if unit has not already fired then roll for ammo now as normal less 1d6). |
| 5 | Tertio or Army Commander hit, Roll a d6: 1-4 Tertio Commander; 5-6 Army Commander (unless it was a Commander testing, then it would be that Commander!) - see chart below. |
| 6 | Sir Gilbert is drunk again! Remove 3 Order Dice for D3 Turns. Note: cumulative in both Dice, up to a maximum of the Commander's Order Dice, and Turns. |
| 7 | Heavy smoke covers front of Regiment for D3 Turns. Half fire Dice, move/charge at half speed, count Soft Cover. This smoke will follow the Regiment around for the duration. |
| 8 | Downgrade – if already Poor, take an immediate Morale Check. |
| 9 | The orders don't make sense. Regiment is now disordered. |
| 10 | Regiment is dismayed and must retire a normal move away from enemy now. They remain in Good Order facing the enemy. |
| 11 | Regiment gets all excited and must advance a normal move towards the enemy now. |
| 12 | Powder replenishment – gain additional d6 powder for one regiment. |
| 13 | Upgrade – if already Excellent then they may make a free move now. |
| 14 | Exceptional Ammunition – for this units next shot in the next turn only (if it is able) double dice before modifiers |
| 15 | Regimental sergeants get shouting – all disordered Regiments in Tertio are now in Good Order; Routers rally but remain Disordered. |
| 16 | Rally back 1 stand to a Regiment in your Tertio. |
| 17 | Rally back 1 stand to a Regiment in your Army |
| 18 | General Advance – all Regiments in the Tertio advance forwards ½ move now. |
| 19 | Any lost Regiment (or lost artillery piece) is brought on as reinforcements at the board edge centre of player's deployment zone. |
| 20 | Reinforcements! Bring on a new unit of your choice (not rare) at the board edge centre of player's deployment zone. |

**Commander Hit Chart – Roll 2d6, effect as follows:**

| | | |
|---|---|---|
| 2-5 | 'E's not pinin', e's passed on! This Commander is no more! He has ceased to be! E's expired and gone to meet his maker! E's a stiff! Etc…… | Roll for new Commander after d3 Turns. |
| 6-9 | Mortal Wound! All right, we'll call it a draw. Oh, oh, I see – running away then! Come back here and take what's coming to you! I'll bite your legs off! | Fights on for d3 Turns, then roll immediately for new Commander. |
| 10-11 | It's only a flesh wound! Commander calls for the barber surgeon. | Out of action for d3 Turns. |
| 12 | 'Tis but a scratch! Commander fights on, earning the admiration of his troops. | Random Regiment under his command is inspired and is upgraded. |

## Example of Shooting

1 unit of 4 stands of musket in demi Herce shoots at medium range at a unit of pike and shot as below:

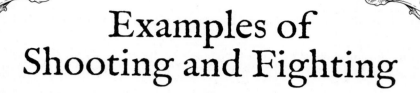

|  |  | PIKE | PIKE |  |  |
|---|---|---|---|---|---|
| SHOT | SHOT | PIKE | PIKE | SHOT | SHOT |

| SHOT | SHOT | SHOT | SHOT |
|---|---|---|---|
| PIKE | PIKE | PIKE | PIKE |

The shooting unit is good and it is its first time shooting:

Number of dice = 2 per stand = 8 dice

+ 1 per 2 stands for being good = 10 dice

The unit has not moved this turn = 10 dice

There are no other factors = 10 dice total

As it is medium range then the unit will need a 5 or 6 to hit.

It throws 4 hits

It then needs a 3, 4, 5 or 6 to kill

It throws 3 kills

It then throws the three kill dice and gets a 1, 2 and 4 – which relates to 2 casualties on the pike element and 1 on the musket element.

This fails to remove a stand so no morale test is required on the impacted unit


# Example of Combat

The same good unit above gets another go (such is the randomness of the dice) and decides to charge.

After testing and passing the order test, the charge move enables it to contact the enemy unit which is in horned battle.

Combat factors:

1 dice per musket stand and 2 dice per pike stand gives 12 dice to each unit.

The attacking unit doubles dice for charging (12 dice) and gets a bonus 1d6 per stand for being good (8 stands = 8 dice) but gains no bonus for pike as they not in the front rank and supported by pike. Total 32 dice!

The defending unit are also good so gain 1d6 per stand bonus (8 stands = 8 dice) and also 2d6 per pike stand in the front rank supported by a stand of pike in good order (2 stands = 4 dice). Total 24 dice.

There are no other modifiers

All dice cause a hit on a 5 or 6.  All Hits cause a Kill on a 3, 4, 5 or 6.

The results are as follows:

The attackers inflict 12 hits and covert 8 to kills – by rethrowing the 8 dice and getting 1,1,3,4,4,5,6,6 3 of these are on pike and 5 on musket – so the defender looses a stand of pike as pike casualties are now 5 and a stand of musket as total musket casualties are now 6.

The defenders inflict 9 hits and convert 5 to kills – 3 kills are on musket and two on pike – there is not a stand lost by the attackers

The defenders now have to take a test for two reasons (loosing a stand and loosing a melee).

The result of this test is that they stand.

The next round of combat is fought immediately…

The attacking unit will now start with 12 dice (2 per pike stand and 1 per musket stand) and also gain 1d6 per base for being good (8 dice). Total 20 dice.

The defending unit will now start with only 9 dice (2 per pike stand and 1 per musket stand) and also gain 2 dice for 1 supported pike stand and also 1 dice per stand for being good (6 dice). Total 17 dice….

## Example of Swirling

In the battles of the English Civil War it was common practice for the Cavalry to be feared by the infantry – who would move into a charge for horse formation. The Cavalry would normally not want to engage with infantry in this formation, however if it could catch them before they had formed this formation the results were usually quite devastating. This lead to the "shiltron" or the "swirling" of the cavalry around the infantry. The rules try to simulate this.

Cavalry unit declares a charge on an infantry unit.

The infantry response is to "Charge for Horse"

The cavalry take an "Order" test and pass it.

The Cavalry then throw their dice for the charge move – getting plenty to contact but not enough to contact within a ½ move so catching the foot on the hop!

The Cavalry are move ½ their move distance towards the defenders and then fire pistols at them.

The result of the pistol fire is 1 pike and 1 shot casualty – but no bases lost – so no morale check.

The defender moves into the charge for horse position.

The cavalry general decides that charging home on a formed block in charge for horse is not worthwhile and so decides to "Swirl" and moves his troops the remaining ½ move around the side of the defender lining itself up for another target.

# Arcs of Fire for Pike and Shot blocks – Horned Battle

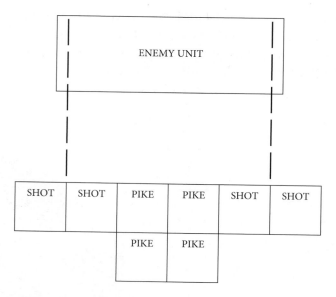

From the above diagram both wings of shot are able to shoot at the enemy unit

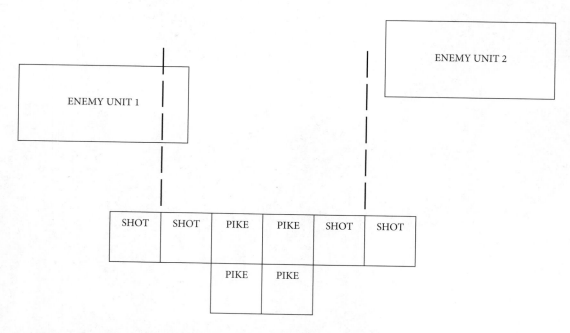

From the above diagram only one wing of shot are able to shoot at the enemy unit.

The right hand wing of shot does not have a legitimate target in its arc so it cannot fire.

## Arcs of Fire for Pike and Shot blocks – Demi Herce

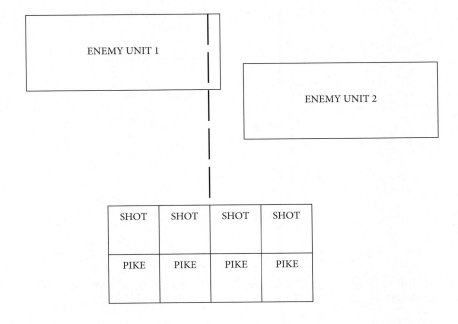

From the above diagram all shot are able to shoot at the enemy unit 1 if in range. No firing is allowed against enemy unit 2 as out of arc.

## Arcs of Fire for Pike and Shot blocks – Charge for Horse

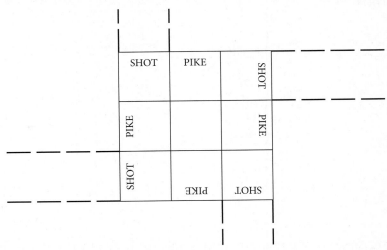

From the above diagram the shooting player may only target one unit that is within range and arc of the shot stands as per their facing direction. This shows the reduced effect of shot in this defensive formation.

## Arcs of Fire for Large Guns, Bows and Darts

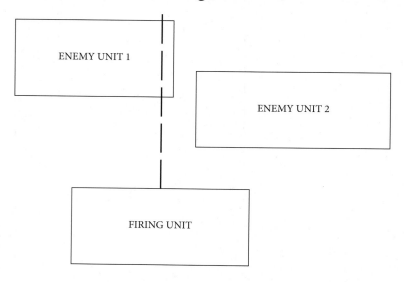

From the above diagram the firing unit is able to shoot at the enemy unit 1 if in range. No firing is allowed against enemy unit 2 as out of arc.

## Arcs of Fire for Large Guns, Bows and Darts

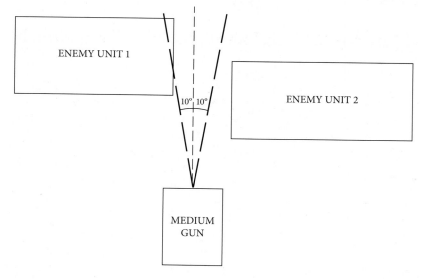

From the above diagram the medium gun is able to shoot at the enemy unit 1 if in range. No firing is allowed against enemy unit 2 as out of arc.

# Arcs of Fire for Small Guns

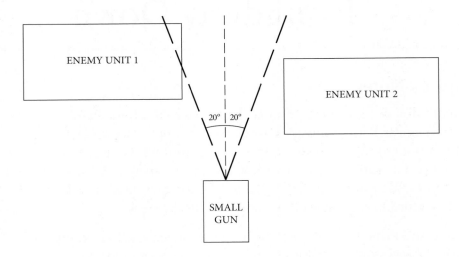

From the above diagram the firing unit is able to shoot at the enemy unit 1 if in range. No firing is allowed against enemy unit 2 as out of arc.

# Arcs of Fire for Pistols

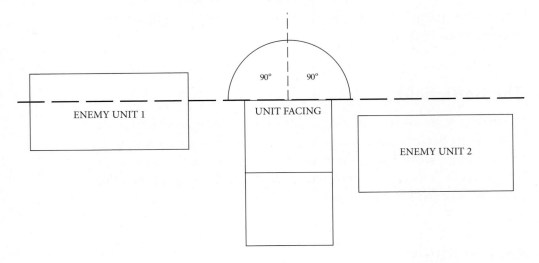

From the above diagram the pistol armed cavalry are able to shoot at the enemy unit 1 if in range. No firing is allowed against enemy unit 2 as out of arc.

# The Battle of Roundway Down

## Umpire's Notes

The battle followed Waller's "drawn" battle with Hopton's army at Lansdowne near Bath. Both sides were short of supply. Hopton, who had been injured in a powder explosion (apparently prisoners were smoking on an ammunition wagon!) withdrew his army to Devizes. Waller followed up and laid siege to the town. Hopton sent his cavalry away to Oxford to request reinforcements to lift the siege.

The King and Prince Rupert were meeting the Queen and her supply train on its' way south so it was left to Maurice, Byron and Wilmot to organise the relief.

Hopton was meant to march out to support the relief upon hearing the signal of two guns firing. He thought this could have been a trap set by Waller and did not march out until much later in the day.

The battle started around noon and lasted until nightfall so a maximum of 10 turns.

## The Battlefield

Set up the table with a low ridge representing Morgan's Hill on one side, which becomes the north, and a rough road representing the Marlborough Road along the eastern edge. The Steep slopes to the rear of Waller's forces are depicted by the southern edge of the table. No hedges or woods are needed.

## Special Rules

Royalist

- Royalist troops are of good quality from the Oxford Army and the two Oxford Brigades will add two to the dice when rolling for

Commander and Regiment ratings however Crawford's troops have been badly handled by Waller in the past and will deduct 1.

Parliamentarian

- Waller is automatically an excellent commander, however the rest of the troops are tired, hungry and thirsty so will deduct one from the commander/Regiment ratings

- Infantry can march while in "charge for horse" at 1D6 per order.

Please see the individual briefing sheets for each side detailing the forces. The game starts with the Royalists deployed on the northern ridge. They have fired their two light guns to signal their arrival to Hopton. Waller is deployed up to 12 Inches from the southern edge.

# Briefing for Prince Maurice

*13 July 1642*

*A messenger has arrived with Crawford's Brigade of Cavalry from Sir Ralph Hopton, commander of your uncle's army in the West of England. He has been forced to retreat to the town of Devizes with his infantry by Sir William Waller. He requests help from your Uncle, King Charles, to lift the siege.*

*Regretfully the King and Prince Rupert are not in Oxford, having gone with much of the Oxford Army to meet the Queen and her convoy of munitions from Holland.*

*After discussion with Lord Byron you decide to attempt lifting the siege. At short notice you are able to raise 2 brigades of horse (3 if you include Crawford's weak brigade). You leave Oxford with 2 Supply wagons and the following forces*

*Lord Byron's Brigade*

- *3 Regiments of horse (16 figures x 3)*

- *1 light gun*

*Wilmot's Brigade*

- *3 Regiments of horse (16 figures x 3)*

- *1 light gun*

*Crawford's Brigade*

- *2 Regiments of Horse (16 figures x 2)*

*You arrive at Morgan's Hill around 2 in the afternoon and deploy on the southern slopes. Your fire the agreed signal (two shots from your light guns) to let Hopton know you have arrived. Waller has obviously had news of your approach and has deployed troops to block your route.*

*Your objective is to clear your way to Devizes and deliver the supplies to Hopton. He will sally up the Marlborough road to meet you.*

# Briefing for William Waller

*13 July 1643, 2 p.m. nightfall at 10 p.m.*

*You have Ralph Hopton's army penned in the town of Devizes. You have driven away his cavalry and are hopeful the town will have to surrender shortly due to lack of supply.*

*Despite a request to the Earl of Essex for him to prevent relief arriving from Oxford, what can only be a Royalist force has been reported coming down the road from Marlborough.*

*Thankfully they have not advanced as rapidly as they could and you have been able to lift the siege and deploy your forces to block their approach. You have left your dragoons to cover any sally in support from the town. Your forces deployed consist of:*

*Waller's Brigade of Horse*

- *3 Regiments of horse (16 figures x 3)*

*Hazelrigg's Brigade of Horse*

- *2 Regiments of horse (16 figures x 2)*
- *1 Regiment of Cuirassiers (16 figures)*

*Popham's Brigade of Foot*

- *2 Regiments of foot (1:1 ratio) (each 4 stands pike, 4 stands shot)*
- *2 light guns*
- *1 medium gun*

*Waller's regiment of dragoons. In front of Devizes. 4 stands of dragoons*

*If you have to retreat you will have to leave the table from the south west corner leading to the Bath road.*

*Your objective is to block the way to Devizes and stop the supplies reaching Hopton…*

# The Battlefield

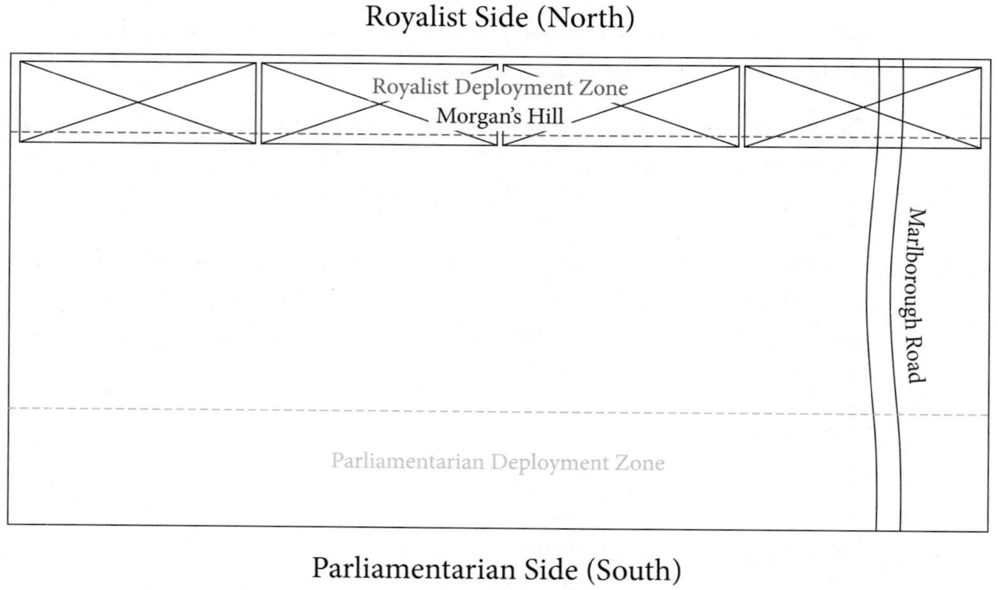

Royalist Side (North)

Royalist Deployment Zone
Morgan's Hill

Marlborough Road

Parliamentarian Deployment Zone

Parliamentarian Side (South)

# Recommended Reading List

Barratt, John, *Cavalier Capital: Oxford in the English Civil War 1642–1646*, Helion 2015

Barratt, John, *Cavaliers: The Royalist Army at War, 1642-1646*, Sutton, 2000

Barratt, John, *Sieges of the English Civil War*, Pen and Sword, 2009

Blackmore, Dr David, *Arms & Armour of the English Civil Wars,* Royal Armouries 1990

Carlton, Charles, *This Seat of Mars: War and the British Isles, 1485-1746*, Yale 2011

Foard, Dr. Glen, *Naseby: The Decisive Campaign*, Leo Cooper, 2004

Henry, Chris, *English Civil War Artillery 1642-51*, Osprey 2005

Louth, Warwick, *The Arte Militaire- The application of 17th Century Military Manuals to Conflict Archaeology*, Helion 2016

Reid, Stuart, *All the King's Armies: A Military History of the English Civil War 1642-1651*, Spellmount 1998

Roberts, Keith, *Ironsides: English Cavalry 1588-1688*, Osprey 2002

Roberts, Keith, *Matchlock Musketeer 1588-1688* Osprey 2002

Roberts, Keith, *Pike and Shot Tactics 1590-1660* Osprey 2010

Scott, Dr. Christopher, Alan Turton & Eric Gruber von Arni *Edgehill: The Battle Reinterpreted*, Pen & Sword 2004

Singleton, Charles, *Famous by My Sword: The Army of Montrose and the Military Revolution*, Helion 2015

Singleton, Charles, *Uncharitable Mischief: Barbarity & Excess in the British Civil Wars*, Pike and Shot Society, 2013

Wanklyn, Professor Malcom, *A Military History of the English Civil War: 1642-1649* Routledge 2004

Wanklyn, Professor Malcom, *Warrior Generals: Winning the British Civil Wars*, Yale 2010

Worton, Dr. Jonathan, *The Battle of Montgomery, 1644 - The English Civil War in the Welsh Borderlands*, Helion 2016

Worton, Dr. Jonathan, *To Settle the Crown - Waging Civil War in Shropshire, 1642-1648*, Helion 2016

Young, Peter, *Edgehill 1642: The campaign and the battle*, Roundwood Press, 1967

Young, Peter, *Marston Moor, 1644: The Campaign and the Battle*, Roundwood Press, 1970

Young, Peter, *Naseby 1645:The Campaign and Battle*, Century, 1985

# The Bicorne Miniatures English Civil War Catalogue

## DESIGNED BY NICK COLLIER AND ALAN MARSH

All these, and more, available from www.bicorne.net

| Historical Commanders | |
|---|---|
| BIC-ECWPF001 | Alexander Leslie Lord Leven |
| BIC-ECWPF002 | Sir Thomas Fairfax |
| BIC-ECWPF003 | Prince Rupert & 'Boy' |
| BIC-ECWPF004 | Sir Philip Stapleton |
| BIC-ECWPF005 | Sir Marmaduke Langsdale |
| BIC-ECWPF006 | Lord Ralph Hopton |
| BIC-ECWPF007 | King Charles I |
| BIC-ECWPF008 | Henry Ireton |
| BIC-ECWPF009 | Prince Maurice |
| BIC-ECWPF010 | Sir William Waller |
| BIC-ECWPF011 | Sir Charles Lucas |
| BIC-ECWPF012 | Lord Ferdinando Fairfax |
| BIC-ECWPF013 | John Hampden |
| BIC-ECWPF014 | Sir Jacob Astley |
| BIC-ECWPF015 | Edward Montagu Earl of Manchester |
| BIC-ECWPF016 | Oliver Cromwell |
| BIC-ECWPF017 | Robert Bertie Earl of Lindsey |
| BIC-ECWPF018 | Robert Devereux Earl of Essex |
| BIC-ECWPF019 | James Graham Marquis of Montrose |
| BIC-ECWPF020 | Sir Edmund Verney |
| BIC-ECWPF021 | Alasdair Mac Colla |
| BIC-ECWPF022 | Edward Massey, Nathaniel Fiennes & Officer of horse |
| BIC-ECWPF023 | King Charles I, Sir Edward Walker & Charles Prince of Wales |

| **Dragoons** | |
|---|---|
| BIC-ECWC008 | Mounted Dragoons (Broad brimmed hats) |
| BIC-ECWC009 | Mounted Dragoons (Helmets) |
| BIC-ECWC010 | Mounted Dragoons (Monteros) |
| BIC-ECWC011 | Mounted Dragoons (Monmouth caps) |
| BIC-ECWC012 | Mounted Dragoon Command (broad brimmed hats) |
| BIC-ECWC013 | Mounted Dragoon Command (Monteros) |
| BIC-ECWC014 | Mounted Dragoon Command (helmets) |
| BIC-ECW032 | Dismounted Dragoons (broad brimmed hats) |
| BIC-ECW033 | Dismounted Dragoons (Monteros) |
| BIC-ECW034 | Dismounted Dragoons (Monmouths) |
| BIC-ECW035 | Dismounted Dragoons (Helmets) - 5 different poses |
| BIC-ECW040 | Dragoon Horse Holders Set 1 |
| BIC-ECW041 | Dragoon Horse Holders & Command Set 2 |
| BIC-ECW042 | Dismounted Dragoon Command |
| **Cavalry** | |
| BIC-ECWC006 | Horse Command 1 |
| BIC-ECWC007 | Horse Command 2 |
| BIC-ECWC028 | King's Life Guard Command |
| BIC-ECWC029 | Cuirassier Command |
| BIC-ECWC001 | Trooper with sword (back & breast plate) Mixed Headgear |
| BIC-ECWC002 | Trooper firing pistol (back & breast plate) Mixed Headgear |
| BIC-ECWC003 | Trooper with sword (buff coat) Mixed Headgear |
| BIC-ECWC004 | Trooper with pistol (buff coat) Mixed Headgear |
| BIC-ECWC005 | Trooper with pistol (doublet) Mixed Headgear |
| BIC-ECWC015 | Trooper with sword (Cassock/Dutch Coat, Soft hats) |
| BIC-ECWC016 | Trooper with sword (Cassock/Dutch Coat, helmets) |
| BIC-ECWC017 | Trooper with pistol (Cassock/Dutch Coat, soft hats) |
| BIC-ECWC018 | Trooper with pistol (Cassock/Dutch Coat, helmets) |
| BIC-ECWC019 | Trooper with carbines held up (buff coat, soft hats) |
| BIC-ECWC020 | Trooper with carbines held up (buff coat, helmets) |
| BIC-ECWC021 | Trooper with carbines held down (buff coat, soft hats) |
| BIC-ECWC022 | Trooper with carbines held down (buff coat, helmets) |

| | |
|---|---|
| BIC-ECWC023 | Trooper King's Life Guard with Sword resting on shoulder |
| BIC-ECWC024 | Trooper King's Life Guard with pistol |
| BIC-ECWC025 | Trooper Cuirassier with Sword |
| BIC-ECWC026 | Trooper Cuirassier with pistol |
| BIC-ECWC027 | Trooper with sword charging (doublet, soft hats) |
| BIC-ECWC030 | Trooper with sword held up, sash, back & breast plate, helmet |
| BIC-ECWC031 | Trooper with sword held down, sash, back & breast plate, helmet |
| BIC-ECWC032 | Trooper with shouldered sword, sash, back & breast plate, helmet |
| **Foot Command** | |
| BIC-ECW016 | Foot Command (Mixed headgear) |
| BIC-ECW017 | Foot Command (helmets & Monteros) |
| BIC-ECW018 | Foot Command (helmets) |
| BIC-ECW019 | Foot Command (Broad brimmed soft hats) |
| BIC-ECW056 | Foot Command standing, tassets, helmets |
| BIC-ECW057 | Foot Command standing, tassets, broad brimmed hats |
| BIC-ECW058 | Foot Command standing, tassets, Monteros |
| **Musketeers** | |
| BIC-ECW011 | Musketeers advancing at port (1) |
| BIC-ECW012 | Musketeers loading |
| BIC-ECW013 | Musketeers at order |
| BIC-ECW014 | Musketeers marching |
| BIC-ECW015 | Musketeers standing firing |
| BIC-ECW020 | Musketeers standing at port |
| BIC-ECW021 | Musketeers standing ramming musket |
| BIC-ECW022 | Musketeers advancing at port (2) |
| BIC-ECW023 | Musketeers loading from bandolier |
| BIC-ECW024 | Musketeers kneeling firing |
| BIC-ECW026 | Musketeers with firelocks at rest Set 1 Broad brimmed hats |
| BIC-ECW027 | Musketeers with firelocks at rest Set 2 Monteros |
| BIC-ECW028 | Musketeers with firelocks at rest Set 3 Monmouths |
| BIC-ECW029 | Musketeers with firelocks at rest Set 4 Helmets |
| BIC-ECW044 | Musketeers with rests marching |
| BIC-ECW045 | Musketeers with rests standing at port |

| | |
|---|---|
| BIC-ECW046 | Musketeers with rests standing firing |
| BIC-ECW049 | Musketeers clubbing & reversed muskets |
| **Pikemen** | |
| BIC-ECW001 | Unarmoured Pikemen at advance |
| BIC-ECW002 | Unarmoured Pikemen at charge |
| BIC-ECW003 | Unarmoured Pikemen at order |
| BIC-ECW004 | Unarmoured Pikemen at shoulder |
| BIC-ECW005 | Unarmoured Pikemen at port |
| BIC-ECW006 | Unarmoured Pikemen marching |
| BIC-ECW007 | Armoured Pikemen at advance |
| BIC-ECW008 | Armoured Pikemen at order |
| BIC-ECW009 | Armoured Pikemen at port |
| BIC-ECW010 | Armoured Pikemen marching |
| BIC-ECW025 | Unarmoured Pikemen ready to receive cavalry |
| BIC-ECW030 | Armoured Pikemen ready to receive cavalry Broad brimmed hats |
| BIC-ECW031 | Armoured Pikemen with tassets ready to receive cavaly |
| BIC-ECW036 | Armoured Pikemen with tassets standing at order |
| BIC-ECW037 | Armoured Pikemen with tassets at port |
| BIC-ECW038 | Armoured Pikemen at charge |
| BIC-ECW047 | Unarmoured Pikemen meleeing with swords |
| BIC-ECW050 | Armoured Pikemen meleeing with swords (8 figures in 4 poses) |
| **Artillery** | |
| BIC-ECWG001 | Cannon |
| BIC-ECWG002 | Demi-Cannon |
| BIC-ECWG003 | Culverin |
| BIC-ECWG004 | Saker |
| BIC-ECWG011 | Minion |
| BIC-ECWG012 | Falcon |
| BIC-ECWG013 | Falconet |
| BIC-ECWG014 | Limber with 4 horses and driver with whip on foot |
| BIC-ECWG017 | Heavy Limber with 4 horses & driver on foot |
| BIC-ECWA001 | Artillery Crew Manouvering/laying gun |
| BIC-ECWA002 | Artillery Crew Loading/firing gun |

| | |
|---|---|
| BIC-ECWA003 | Scots Artillery Crew loading/firing |
| BIC-ECWA004 | Scots Artillery Crew Manouvering gun |
| BIC-ECWA005 | Artillery Crew Loading/firing |
| BIC-ECWA006 | Artillery Crew Manouvering gun |
| BIC-ECWG018 | Mortar & 3 crew |
| BIC-ECWG005 | Frame Gun with 3 crew (soft hats) firing |
| BIC-ECWG006 | Frame Gun with 3 crew (soft hats) loading |
| BIC-ECWG007 | Frame Gun with 3 crew (soft hats) & mule manouvering |
| BIC-ECWG008 | Frame Gun with 3 Scots crew (bonnets) firing |
| BIC-ECWG009 | Frame Gun with 3 Scots crew (bonnets) loading |
| BIC-ECWG010 | Frame Gun with 3 Scots crew (bonnets) & mule manouvering |

### Covenanter Dragoons

| | |
|---|---|
| BIC-ECWS031 | Covenanter Dismounted Dragoons |
| BIC-ECWSC008 | Covenanter Mounted Dragoon Command |
| BIC-ECWSC006 | Covenanter Mounted Dragoons set 1 |
| BIC-ECWSC007 | Covenanter Mounted Dragoons set 2 |

### Covenanter Cavalry

| | |
|---|---|
| BIC-ECWSC005 | Covenanter Cavalry command |
| BIC-ECWSC001 | Covenanter Lancer in bonnets |
| BIC-ECWSC002 | Covenanter Lancer in helmets |
| BIC-ECWSC003 | Covenanter Trooper with sword |
| BIC-ECWSC004 | Covenanter Trooper with pistol |

### Covenanter Foot Command

| | |
|---|---|
| BIC-ECWS030 | Covenanter Foot Command Set 2 |
| BIC-ECWS029 | Covenanter Foot Command Set 1 |

### Covenanter Pikemen

| | |
|---|---|
| BIC-ECWS007 | Covenanter Pikeman at charge |
| BIC-ECWS008 | Covenanter Pikeman at order Set 1 |
| BIC-ECWS009 | Covenanter Pikeman at order Set 2 |
| BIC-ECWS010 | Covenanter Pikeman at advance |
| BIC-ECWS011 | Covenanter Pikeman marching at shoulder |
| BIC-ECWS012 | Covenanter Pikeman at port |
| BIC-ECWS027 | Covenanter Pikeman ready to receive cavalry |

| Covenanter Musketeers | |
|---|---|
| BIC-ECWS001 | Covenanter Musketeer standing firing |
| BIC-ECWS002 | Covenanter Musketeer ramming musket |
| BIC-ECWS003 | Covenanter Musketeer marching |
| BIC-ECWS004 | Covenanter Musketeer at order |
| BIC-ECWS005 | Covenanter Musketeer standing at port |
| BIC-ECWS006 | Covenanter Musketeer advancing |
| BIC-ECWS028 | Covenanter Musketeer kneeling firing |
| **Scots Highlanders** | |
| BIC-ECWS026 | Highlander Command |
| BIC-ECWS013 | Highlander Bowman taking arrow from ground |
| BIC-ECWS014 | Highlander Bowman firing bow |
| BIC-ECWS015 | Highlander Bowman putting arrow into bow |
| BIC-ECWS016 | Highlander Bowman drawing arrow from quiver |
| BIC-ECWS017 | Highlander Bowman standing at order with bow |
| BIC-ECWS018 | Highlander Bowman advancing |
| BIC-ECWS019 | Highlander Standing with sword and shield |
| BIC-ECWS020 | Highlander Charging with sword up and shield |
| BIC-ECWS021 | Highlander Charging with sword down and shield |
| BIC-ECWS022 | Highlander at Order with Lochaber Axe |
| BIC-ECWS023 | Highlander Charging with lochaber axe |
| BIC-ECWS024 | Highlander Standing firing musket |
| BIC-ECWS025 | Highlander Kneeling firing musket |
| **Irish** | |
| BIC-ECWIR001 | Irish Musketeers standing firing |
| BIC-ECWIR002 | Irish Musketeers at order |
| BIC-ECWIR003 | Irish Musketeers at port |
| BIC-ECWIR004 | Irish Musketeers advancing at port |
| BIC-ECWIR005 | Irish Musketeers marching |
| BIC-ECWIR006 | Irish Pikemen at order |
| BIC-ECWIR007 | Irish Pikemen at advance |
| BIC-ECWIR008 | Irish Pikemen at port |
| BIC-ECWIR009 | Irish Pikemen at charge |

| Wagons and Civilians | |
|---|---|
| BIC-ECWG015 | 4 wheeled wagon with 1 horse & driver with whip on foot |
| BIC-ECWG016 | 2 wheeled cart with 1 horse & driver with whip on foot |
| BIC-ECW039 | Villagers |
| BIC-ECW048 | Casualties |
| BIC-ECW043 | Peasants Advancing |
| BIC-ECW051 | Sappers/Engineers |
| BIC-ECW052 | Prisoners |
| **Equipment** | |
| BIC-S1 | Finials & cords (flag tops) plus poles |
| BIC-ECWP10 | 4" Wire Pikes (24) |
| BIC-ECWG019 | Pack of Muskets |
| BIC-ECWG020 | Pack of Barrels |
| BIC-ECWG021 | Pack of Sacks |
| BIC-ECWG022 | Pack of Farm Implements |
| BIC-ECWG023 | Pack of Powder Barrels |
| BIC-ECWG024 | Pack of Halberds |
| BIC-ECWG025 | Pack of Partizans |
| BIC-ECWG026 | Pack of Lochaber Axes |
| BIC-ECWG027 | Pack of bows |
| BIC-ECWG028 | Pack of Highland shields |
| BIC-ECWG029 | Pack of Wooden boxes |
| BIC-ECWG030 | Pack of cannon ball stacks |
| BIC-ECWG031 | Pack of Artillery Tools |

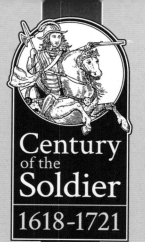

# Century of the Soldier 1618-1721

# THE CENTURY OF THE SOLDIER SERIES
## WARFARE c1618-1721

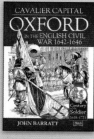

The 'Century of the Soldier' series covers the period of military history c. 1618–1721, the 'golden era' of Pike and Shot warfare.

This time frame has been seen by many historians as a period of not only great social change, but of fundamental developments within military matters. This is the period of the 'military revolution', the development of standing armies, the widespread introduction of black powder weapons and a greater professionalism within the culture of military personnel. The series will examine the period in a greater degree of detail than has hitherto been attempted, and has a very wide brief, with the intention of covering all aspects of the period from the battles, campaigns, logistics and tactics, to the personalities, armies, uniforms and equipment.

*Find out more and order online at*
## www.helion.co.uk/centuryofthesoldier

  helionbooks     blog.helion.co.uk     Century-of-the-Soldier

# HELION & COMPANY

www.helion.co.uk    0121 705 3393    info@helion.co.uk

*One of the world's leading specialist publishers and booksellers of military history*